THE CONTEMPORARY SHAKESPEARE

Edited by A.L. Rowse

As You Like It

Modern Text with Introduction

UNIVERSITY PRESS OF AMERICA

University Press of America,™ Inc.

4720 Boston Way
Lanham, MD 20706

3 Henrietta Street
London WC2E 8LU England

Distributed to the trade by The Scribner Book Companies

Library of Congress Cataloging in Publication Data

Shakespeare, William, 1564-1616.
  As you like it.

  (The Contemporary Shakespeare)
  I. Rowse, A.L. (Alfred Leslie), 1903-
II. Title. III. Series: Shakespeare, William, 1564-1616.
Plays (University Press of America : Pbk. ed.)
PR2803.A2R64   1984 c.2 822.3'3   84-15393
ISBN 0-8191-3914-9 (pbk.)

This play is also available as part of Volume II in a six volume clothbound
and slipcased set.

Book design by Leon Bolognese

WHY A CONTEMPORARY SHAKESPEARE?

The starting point of my project was when I learned both from television and in education, that Shakespeare is being increasingly dropped in schools and colleges because of the difficulty of the language. In some cases, I gather, they are given just a synopsis of the play, then the teacher or professor embroiders from his notes.

This is deplorable. We do not want Shakespeare progressively dropped because of superfluous difficulties that can be removed, skilfully, conservatively, keeping to every line of the text. Nor must we look at the question statically, for this state of affairs will worsen as time goes on and we get further away from the language of 400 years ago—difficult enough in all conscience now.

We must begin by ridding our mind of prejudice, i.e. we must not pre-judge the matter. A friend of mine on New York radio said that he was 'appalled' at the very idea; but when he heard my exposition of what was proposed he found it reasonable and convincing.

3

Just remember, I do not need it myself: *I live in the Elizabethan age*, Shakespeare's time, and have done for years, and am familiar with its language, and his. But even for me there are still difficulties—still more for modern people, whom I am out to help.

Who, precisely?

Not only students at school and in college, but all readers of Shakespeare. Not only those, but all viewers of the plays, in the theatre, on radio and television—actors too, who increasingly find pronunciation of the words difficult, particularly obsolete ones—and there are many, besides the difficulty of accentuation.

The difficulties are naturally far greater for non-English-speaking peoples. We must remember that he is our greatest asset, and that other peoples use him a great deal in learning our language. There are no Iron Curtains for him—though, during Mao's Cultural Revolution in China, he was prohibited. Now that the ban has been lifted, I learn that the Chinese in thousands flock to his plays.

Now, a good deal that was grammatical four hundred years ago is positively ungrammatical today. We might begin by removing what is no longer good grammar.

For example: plural subjects with a verb in the singular:

'*Is* Bushy, Green and the earl of Wiltshire dead?' Any objection to replacing 'is' correctly by 'are'? Certainly not. I notice that some modern editions already correct—

These high wild hills and rough uneven ways

Draws out our miles and makes them wearisome

to 'draw' and 'make', quite sensibly. Then, why not go further and regularise this Elizabethan usage to modern, consistently throughout?

Similarly with archaic double negatives—'Nor shall you not think neither'—and double comparatives: 'this

is more worser than before.' There are hundreds of instances of what is now just bad grammar to begin with.

There must be a few thousand instances of superfluous subjunctives to reduce to simplicity and sense. Today we use the subjunctive occasionally after 'if', when
we say 'if it be'. But we mostly say today 'if it is'. Now
Shakespeare has hundreds of subjunctives, not only
after if, but after though, although, unless, lest,
whether, until, till, etc.

I see no point whatever in retaining them. They only
add superfluous trouble in learning English, when the
great appeal of our language as a world-language is
precisely that it has less grammar to learn than almost
any. Russian is unbelievably complicated. Inflected
languages—German is like Latin in this respect—are
really rather backward; it has been a great recommendation that English has been more progressive in this
respect in simplifying itself.

Now we can go further along this line: keep a few subjunctives, if you must, but reduce them to a minimum.

Let us come to the verb. It is a great recommendation
to modern English that our verbs are comparatively
simple to conjugate—unlike even French, for example.
In the Elizabethan age there was a great deal more of
it, and some of it inconsistent in modern usage. Take
Shakespeare's,

'Where is thy husband now? Where be thy brothers?'

Nothing is lost by rendering this as we should today:

Where is your husband now? Where are your brothers?

And so on.

The second and third person singular—all those
shouldsts and wouldsts, wilts and shalts, haths and
doths, have become completely obsolete. Here a vast

simplification may be effected—with no loss as far as I can see, and with advantages from several points of view.

For example, 'st' at the end of a word is rather difficult to say, and more difficult even for us when it is succeeded by a word beginning with 'th'. Try saying, 'Why usurpedst thou this?' Foreigners have the greatest difficulty in pronouncing our 'th' anyway—many never succeed in getting it round their tongues. Many of these tongue-twisters even for us proliferate in Shakespeare, and I see no objection to getting rid of *superfluous* difficulties. Much easier for people to say, 'Why did you usurp this?'—the same number of syllables too.

This pre-supposes getting rid of almost all thous and thees and thines. I have no objection to keeping a few here and there, if needed for a rhyme—even then they are sometimes not necessary.

Some words in Shakespeare have changed their meaning into the exact opposite: we ought to remove that stumbling-block. When Hamlet says, 'By heaven, I'll make a ghost of him that *lets* me', he means *stops*; and we should replace it by stops, or holds me. Shakespeare regularly uses the word 'owe' where we should say own: the meaning has changed. Take a line like, 'Thou dost here usurp the name thou ow'st not': we should say, 'You do here usurp the name you own not', with the bonus of getting rid of two ugly 'sts'.

The word 'presently' in the Elizabethan age did not mean in a few minutes or so, but immediately—instantly has the same number of syllables. 'Prevent' then had its Latin meaning, to go before, or forestall. Shakespeare frequently uses the word 'still' for always or ever.

Let us take the case of many archaic forms of words, simple one-syllable words that can be replaced without the slightest difference to the scansion: 'sith' for since, 'wrack' for wreck, 'holp' for helped, 'writ' for wrote, 'brake' for broke, 'spake' for spoke, 'bare' for bore, etc.

These give no trouble, nor do a lot of other words that he uses: 'repeal' for recall, 'reproof' for disproof, 'decline' for incline. A few words do give more trouble. The linguistic scholar, C. T. Onions, notes that it is sometimes difficult to give the precise meaning Shakespeare attaches to the word 'conceit'; it usually means thought, or fancy, or concept. I do not know that it ever has our meaning; actually the word 'conceited' with him means ingenious or fantastic, as 'artificial' with Elizabethans meant artistic or ingenious.

There is a whole class of words that have completely gone out, of which moderns do not know the meaning. I find no harm in replacing the word 'coistrel' by rascal, which is what it means—actually it has much the same sound—or 'coil' by fuss; we find 'accite' for summon, 'indigest' for formless. Hamlet's word 'reechy', for the incestuous kisses of his mother and her brother-in-law, has gone out of use: the nearest word, I suppose, would be reeky, but filthy would be a suitable modern equivalent.

In many cases it is extraordinary how little one would need to change, how conservative one could be. Take Hamlet's famous soliloquy, 'To be or not to be.' I find only two words that moderns would not know the meaning of, and one of those we might guess:

>   . . .When he himself might his *quietus* make
>   With a bare bodkin? Who would *fardels* bear. . .

'Quietus' means put paid; Elizabethans wrote the Latin 'quietus est' at the bottom of a bill that was paid—when it was—to say that it was settled. So that you could replace 'quietus' by settlement, same number of syllables, though not the same accentuation; so I would prefer to use the word acquittance, which has both.

'Fardels' means burdens; I see no objection to rendering,
'Who would burdens bear'—same meaning, same number
of syllables, same accent: quite simple. I expect all the
ladies to know what a bodkin is: a long pin, or skewer.

Now let us take something really difficult—perhaps
the most difficult passage to render in all Shakespeare. It
is the virtuoso comic piece describing all the diseases
that horseflesh is heir to, in *The Taming of the Shrew*.
The horse is Petruchio's. President Reagan tells me that
this is the one Shakespearean part that he played—and a
very gallant one too. In Britain last year we saw a fine
performance of his on horseback in Windsor Park along-
side of Queen Elizabeth II—very familiar ground to
William Shakespeare and Queen Elizabeth I, as we know
from *The Merry Wives of Windsor*.

Here is a headache for us: Petruchio's horse (not President Reagan's steed) was 'possessed with the glanders,
and like to mose in the chine; troubled with the lampass,
infected with the fashions, full of windgalls, sped with
spavins, rayed with the yellows, past cure of the fives,
stark spoiled with the staggers, begnawn with the bots;
swayed in the back, and shoulder-shotten; near-legged
before, and with a half-cheeked bit, and a headstall of
sheep's leather', etc.

What on earth are we to make of that? No doubt it raised
a laugh with Elizabethans, much more familiarly acquainted with horseflesh than we are; but I doubt if
Hollywood was able to produce a nag for Reagan that
qualified in all these respects.

Now, even without his horsemanship, we can clear
one fence at the outset: 'mose in the chine'. Pages of
superfluous commentary have been devoted to that word
'mose'. There was no such Elizabethan word: it was
simply a printer's misprint for 'mourn', meaning drip-
ping or running; so it suggests a running sore. You would

need to consult the *Oxford English Dictionary*, compiled on historical lines, for some of the words, others like 'glanders' country folk know and we can guess.

So I would suggest a rendering something like this: 'possessed with glanders, and with a running sore in the back; troubled in the gums, and infected in the glands; full of galls in the fetlocks and swollen in the joints; yellow with jaundice, past cure of the strangles; stark spoiled with the staggers, and gnawed by worms; swayed in the back and shoulder put out; near-legged before, and with a half-cheeked bit and headgear of sheep's leather', etc. That at least makes it intelligible.

Oddly enough, one encounters the greatest difficulty with the least important words and phrases, Elizabethan expletives and malapropisms, or salutations like God 'ild you, Godden, for God shield you, Good-even, and so on. 'God's wounds' was Elizabeth I's favourite swearword; it appears frequently enough in Victorian novels as 'Zounds'— I have never heard anyone use it. The word 'Marry!', as in the phrase 'Marry come up!' has similarly gone out, though a very old gentleman at All Souls, Sir Charles Oman, had heard the phrase in the back-streets of Oxford just after the 1914-18 war. 'Whoreson' is frequent on the lips of coarse fellows in Shakespeare: the equivalent in Britain today would be bloody, in America (I suppose) s.o.b.

Relative pronouns, who and which: today we use who for persons, which for things. In Elizabethan times the two were hardly distinguished and were interchangeable. Provokingly Shakespeare used the personal relative 'who' more frequently for impersonal objects, rivers, buildings, towns; and then he no less frequently uses 'which' for persons. This calls out to be regularised for the modern reader.

Other usages are more confusing. The word 'cousin'

was used far more widely by the Elizabethans for their kin: it included nephews, for instance. Thus it is confusing in the English History plays to find a whole lot of nephews—like Richard III's, whom he had made away with in the Tower of London—referred to and addressed as cousins. That needs regularisation today, in the interests of historical accuracy and to get the relationship clear. The word 'niece' was sometimes used of a grandchild—in fact this is the word Shakespeare used in his will for his little grand-daughter Elizabeth, his eventual heiress who ended up as Lady Barnard, leaving money to her poor relations the Hathaways at Stratford. The Latin word *neptis*, from which niece comes also meant grandchild—Shakespeare's grammar-school education at Stratford was in Latin, and this shows you that he often thought of a word in terms of its Latin derivation.

Malapropisms, misuse of words, sometimes mistaking of meanings, are frequent with uneducated people, and sometimes not only with those. Shakespeare transcribed them from lower-class life to raise a laugh, more frequently than any writer for the purpose. They are an endearing feature of the talk of Mistress Quickly, hostess of the Boar's Inn in East Cheapside, and we have no difficulty in making out what she means. But in case some of us do, and for the benefit of non-native English speakers, I propose the correct word in brackets afterwards: 'You have brought her into such a canaries [quandary]. . .and she's as fartuous [virtuous] a civil, modest wife. . .'

Abbreviations: Shakespeare's text is starred—and in my view, marred—by innumerable abbreviations, which not only look ugly on the page but are sometimes difficult to pronounce. It is not easy to pronounce 'is't', or 'in't', or 'on't', and some others: if we cannot get rid of them altogether they should be drastically reduced. Similarly with 'i'th'', 'o'th'', with which the later plays are liberally bespattered, for "in the" or "of the."

We also have a quite unnecessary spattering of apostrophes in practically all editions of the plays—''d' for the past participle, e.g. 'gather'd'. Surely it is much better to regularise the past participle 'ed', e.g. gathered; and when the last syllable is, far less frequently, to be pronounced, then accent it, gatherèd.

This leads into the technical question of scansion, where a practising poet is necessary to get the accents right, to help the reader, and still more the actor. Most people will hardly notice that, very often, the frequent ending of words in 'ion', like reputation, has to be pronounced with two syllables at the end. So I propose to accent this when necessary, e.g. reputatiòn. I have noticed the word 'ocean' as tri-syllabic, so I accent it, to help, oceàn. A number of words which to us are monosyllables were pronounced as two: hour, fire, tired; I sometimes accent or give them a dieresis, either hoùr or fïre. In New England speech words like prayèr, thëre, are apt to be pronounced as two syllables—closer to Elizabethan usage (as with words like gotten) than is modern speech in Britain.

What I notice in practically all editions of Shakespeare's plays is that the editors cannot be relied on to put the accents in the right places. One play edited by a well known Shakespearean editor had, I observed, a dozen accents placed over the wrong syllables. This is understandable, for these people don't write poetry and do not know how to scan. William Shakespeare knew all about scanning, and you need to be both familiar with Elizabethan usage and a practising traditional poet to be able to follow him.

His earlier verse was fairly regular in scansion, mostly iambic pentameter with a great deal of rhyme. As time went on he loosened out, until there are numerous irregular lines—this leaves us much freer in the matter of modernising. Our equivalents should be rhythmically as close as possible, but a strait-jacket need be no part of the equipment. A good Shakespearean scholar tells us, 'there is no necessity for Shakespeare's lines to scan absolutely. He thought of his verse as spoken rather than written and of his rhythmic units in terms of the voice rather than the page.'

There is nothing exclusive or mandatory about my project. We can all read Shakespeare in any edition we like—in the rebarbative olde Englishe spelling of the First Folio, if we wish. Any number of conventional academic editions exist, all weighed down with a burden of notes, many of them superfluous. I propose to make most of them unnecessary—only one occasionally at the foot of very few pages. Let the text be freed of superfluous difficulties, remove obstacles to let it speak for itself, while adhering conservatively to every line.

We really do not need any more editions of the Plays on conventional lines—more than enough of those exist already. But *A Contemporary Shakespeare* on these lines—both revolutionary and conservative—should be a help to everybody all round the world—though especially for younger people, increasingly with time moving away from the language of 400 years ago.

INTRODUCTION

T his gay and beautiful play is the last of Shakespeare's light-hearted comedies. After this the
scene clouds over in the life of the time, which
Shakespeare so richly and faithfully reflected. He was very
much a man of his time, his career a characteristic
Elizabethan success story. His response to the time, its
most sensitive register, was an important element in his
success, as with any professional man of the theatre.

The year is 1598, the beginning of the Irish war led by the
great O'Neill, which harassed the last years of Elizabeth I's
reign and ruined Essex (among others). There is a tell-tale
change Shakespeare made from the source of his play,
Thomas Lodge's *Rosalynde, Euphues' Golden Legacie*.
Lodge had written, 'thou barkest with the wolves of Syria
against the moon'; Shakespeare altered this to 'the howling
of *Irish* wolves against the moon.' So much for those who
cannot see how closely this man of the theatre was in touch
with what was going on.

Several other touches bring this home to us. This year
saw the publication at last of Marlowe's poem *Hero and
Leander*, which he had been writing in competition with
Shakespeare's *Venus and Adonis* for Southhampton's
patronage but left unfinished when he was killed in May
1593. Its publication brought back memories of that close
association, about which we should like to know more.
Several references bring back the memory of the brilliant
tragic Marlowe, including the famous couplet in which

Shakespeare virtually salutes him by name—the only time he specifically quotes a line from a contemporary:

Dead shepherd, now I find thy saw [phrase] of might:
'Who ever loved that loved not at first sight?'

We have a passage about Hero and Leander made fun of. Rosalind, disguised as a youth, takes the name of Ganymede—the first scene of Marlowe's *Dido* had depicted him being dandled on Jove's knee. Marlowe's end in the little room of the tavern at Deptford had been over a quarrel about 'le reckoning', according to the inquest—corroborated by Shakespeare in the phrase about the stupidity that 'strikes a man more dead than a great reckoning in a little room.'

The voyages, so prominent at the time are no less in mind. Rosalind has an image drawn from them: 'an inch of delay' in learning about her Orlando is 'a South Sea of discovery'. The Pacific was the South Sea to the Elizabethans who made the first English voyages into it. Her love 'has an unknown bottom, like the Bay of Portugal', familiar to them but unplumbed. Jacques considers Touchstone's brain 'as dry as the remainder biscuit after a voyage'.

Even Rosalind's image, 'I will weep for nothing, like Diana in the fountain' has its contemporary reference that would appeal to the audience. For only a couple of years before a statue of Diana was set up at the cross in Cheapside, water from the Thames 'prilling from her naked breast.' The statue was as familiar to Shakespeare himself, for about this time he was lodging in the parish of St. Helen's, Bishopsgate. In this parish too lived the composer of the music for 'It was a lover and his lass', Thomas Morley, the delightful madrigalist.

The literary references no less bring back the time. A most influential book was the dramatist Lyly's *Euphues*, with its inflated rhetorical style, which caught on and was carried on by Lodge in his *Rosalynde, Euphues' Golden*

Legacie. This is made fun of—its emptiness, saying nothing—by Touchstone the Clown: 'to have is to have: for it is a figure in rhetoric that drink, being poured out of a cup into a glass, by filling the one does empty the other.' Touchstone also takes up a line from Philip Sidney, the first of the Sonnets, *Astrophil to Stella*.

Actually, the role of a jester—which was much to the fore in great houses and at Court—is that which has most dated and appeals less to us with the verbal exchanges, the puns and plays on words, to which Shakespeare was so much addicted and which appealed so strongly to Elizabethans. Sir William Davenant, who knew, described him as 'a prodigious wit', which meant then prodigiously 'clever': though this is obvious, it is an aspect of the man not often mentioned. This play has a discussion on the role of a Fool and the place of Folly, between the disillusioned cynical Jaques and Touchstone, whose part would have been taken by the popular Will Kemp, still with the Lord Chamberlain's Company.

The leading parts of Rosalind and Celia were taken by two boy-actors, the first tall and fair, the second short and dark. Rosalind speaks the Epilogue—a very personal one —in person as a boy: "If I were a woman, I would kiss as many of you as had beards that pleased me', etc. An early tradition tells us that Shakespeare played the part of the old man, Adam. We must always remember—our leading authority, G. E. Bentley, instructs us—how he adapted the parts in his plays to the personnel at command in his Company.

What appeals most to us today is what probably appealed most to Shakespeare. The play is about love and love-making—he is our greatest poet of love; and it all takes place in the Forest of Arden, his own native Warwickshire in mind. There are the shepherds and the sheepcotes of the Cotswolds, the valley bottoms and streams bordered with osiers; the country folk, William and Audrey, Corin, Silvius and Phebe; a poor vicar in Martext—with its reflection of the contemporary Marprelate controversy (in which Nashe took some part).

Shakespeare deepens the scene by contrasting the pastoral life of the Forest with the insincerities and treacheries of the Court. For the play is set going by the rightful Duke having been displaced by his brother. In this idyllic Forest life—there is nostalgia in it—'they fleet the time carelessly, as they did in the golden world.' Rusticated duke, lords turned foresters, Court ladies taking to the woods, shepherds and shepherdesses—the rough-and-tumble of real life has the consolations of the imagination, 'Under the greenwood tree.' No wonder Thomas Hardy took it for the title of his early pastoral novel—Shakespeare having the providential gift of inspiring creativity in others.

The text of this play, from the First Folio, is a good one and offers few difficulties. Nor has it been necessary to modernise many words; some few have changed their meaning in four hundred years, e.g. 'expediently' for immediately, 'humourous' for moody, 'conceit' for thought or fancy. Few archaic words appear, e.g. 'carlot' for peasant; 'intendment' was Shakespeare's coinage for intention.

CHARACTERS

DUKE SENIOR

DUKE FREDERICK, his brother and usurper

AMIENS
JAQUES } lords attending on Duke Senior

OLIVER, eldest son of Sir Rowland de Boys

JAQUES
ORLANDO } younger sons of Sir Rowland de Boys

LE BEAU, a courtier attending on Duke Frederick

CHARLES, a wrestler

ADAM, an old servant to Sir Rowland de Boys

DENNIS, a servant

TOUCHSTONE, a clown

SIR OLIVER MARTEXT, a country vicar

CORIN
SILVIUS } shepherds

WILLIAM, a country fellow

HYMEN, god of marriage

ROSALIND, daughter of Duke Senior

CELIA, daughter of Duke Frederick

PHEBE, a shepherdess

AUDREY, a country girl

LORDS, PAGES, and ATTENDANTS

Scene: Oliver's orchard; Duke Frederick's Court, the Forest of Arden

Act I

❀

SCENE I
An orchard.

Enter ORLANDO *and* ADAM.

ORLANDO As I remember, Adam, it was upon this fashion bequeathed me by will but a poor thousand crowns, and, as you say, charged my brother on his blessing to breed me well: and there begins my sadness. My brother Jaques he keeps at school, and report speaks goldenly of his profit. For my part, he keeps me rustically at home or, to speak more properly, stays me here at home unkept: for call you that keeping for a gentleman of my birth that differs not from the stalling of an ox? His horses are bred better, for, besides that they are fair with their feeding, they are taught their manage, and to that end riders dearly hired. But I, his brother, gain nothing under him but growth, for which his animals on his dunghills are as much bound to him as I. Besides this nothing that he so plentifully gives me, the something that nature gave me his countenance seems to take from me. He lets me feed with his hinds, bars me the place of a brother, and, as much as in him lies, mines my gentility with my education. This is it, Adam, that grieves me; and the spirit of my father, which I think is within me, begins to mutiny against this servitude. I will no longer endure it, though yet I know no wise remedy how to avoid it.

Enter OLIVER.

ADAM   Yonder comes my master, your brother.

ORLANDO   Go apart, Adam, and you shall hear how he
will shake me up.

OLIVER   Now, sir, what make you here?

ORLANDO   Nothing. I am not taught to make anything.

OLIVER   What mar you then, sir?

ORLANDO   Sir, I am helping you to mar that which God
made, a poor unworthy brother of yours, with idleness.

OLIVER   Sir, be better employed, and be naught awhile.

ORLANDO   Shall I keep your hogs and eat husks with
them? What prodigal portion have I spent that I should
come to such penury?

OLIVER   Know you where you are, sir?

ORLANDO   O, sir, very well: here in your orchard.

OLIVER   Know you before whom, sir?

ORLANDO   Ay, better than him I am before knows me. I
know you are my eldest brother, and in the gentle
condition of blood you should so know me. The courtesy
of nations allows you my better in that you are the first
born, but the same tradition takes not away my blood
were there twenty brothers between us. I have as much
of my father in me as you, albeit I confess your coming
before me is nearer to his reverence.

OLIVER   What, boy!

[Strikes him.]

ORLANDO   Come, come, elder brother, you are too
young in this.

[Holds him.]

OLIVER   Will you lay hands on me, villain?

ORLANDO   I am no villain. I am the youngest son of Sir
Rowland de Boys; he was my father, and he is thrice a

villain that says such a father begot villains. Were you not
my brother, I would not take this hand from your throat
till this other had pulled out your tongue for saying so.
You have railed on yourself.

ADAM   Sweet masters, be patient: for your father's remem-
brance, be at accord.

OLIVER   Let me go, I say.

ORLANDO   I will not till I please. You shall hear me. My
father charged you in his will to give me good education:
you have trained me like a peasant, obscuring and hiding
from me all gentlemanlike qualities. The spirit of my
father grows strong in me, and I will no longer endure it.
Therefore allow me such exercises as may become a
gentleman, or give me the poor lot my father left me by
testament. With that I will go buy my fortunes.

OLIVER   And what will you do? beg when that is spent?
Well, sir, get you in. I will not long be troubled with you.
You shall have some part of your will. I pray you leave me.

ORLANDO   I will no further offend you than becomes me
for my good.

OLIVER   Get you with him, you old dog.

ADAM   Is 'old dog' my reward? Most true, I have lost my
teeth in your service. God be with my old master; he
would not have spoken such a word.

Exeunt Orlando, Adam.

OLIVER   Is it even so? Begin you to grow upon me? I will
physic your rankness and yet give no thousand crowns
either. Holla, Dennis!

Enter DENNIS.

DENNIS   Calls your worship?

OLIVER   Was not Charles the Duke's wrestler here to
speak with me?

DENNIS   So please you, he is here at the door and
importunes access to you.

OLIVER   Call him in. *[Exit* DENNIS.*]* It will be a good
way; and to-morrow the wrestling is.

Enter CHARLES.

CHARLES   Good morrow to your worship.

OLIVER   Good Monsieur Charles, what's the new news
at the new court?

CHARLES   There's no news at the court, sir, but the old
news: that is, the old Duke is banished by his younger
brother the new Duke, and three or four loving lords have
put themselves into voluntary exile with him, whose
lands and revenues enrich the new Duke. Therefore he
gives them good leave to wander.

OLIVER   Can you tell if Rosalind, the Duke's daughter, is
banished with her father?

CHARLES   O, no; for the Duke's daughter her cousin so
loves her, being ever from their cradles bred together, that
she would have followed her exile, or have died to stay
behind her. She is at the court, and no less beloved of her
uncle than his own daughter, and never two ladies loved
as they do.

OLIVER   Where will the old Duke live?

CHARLES   They say he is already in the Forest of Arden,
and many merry men with him; and there they live like
the old Robin Hood of England. They say many young
gentlemen flock to him every day, and fleet the time
carelessly as they did in the golden world.

OLIVER   What, you wrestle to-morrow before the new
Duke?

CHARLES   Sure, do I, sir; and I came to acquaint you with
a matter. I am given, sir, secretly to understand that your
younger brother, Orlando, has a disposition to come in
disguised against me to try a fall. To-morrow, sir, I wrestle
for my credit, and he that escapes me without some
broken limb shall acquit him well. Your brother is but
young and tender, and for your love I would be loth to
throw him, as I must for my own honor if he comes in.
Therefore, out of my love to you, I came hither to
acquaint you that either you might stay him from his

intention, or brook such disgrace well as he shall run into, in that it is a thing of his own search and altogether against my will.

OLIVER Charles, I thank you for your love to me, which you shall find I will most kindly requite. I had myself notice of my brother's purpose herein and have by underhand means labored to dissuade him from it; but he is resolute. I'll tell you, Charles, it is the stubbornest young fellow of France; full of ambition, an envious emulator of every man's good parts, a secret and villainous contriver against me his natural brother. Therefore use your discretion. I had as soon you did break his neck as his finger. And you were best look to it; for if you do him any slight disgrace, or if he does not mightily grace himself on you, he will practise against you by poison, entrap you by some treacherous device, and never leave you till he has taken your life by some indirect means or other. For I assure you, and almost with tears I speak it, there is not one so young and so villainous this day living. I speak but brotherly of him, but should I anatomize him to you as he is, I must blush and weep, and you must look pale and wonder.

CHARLES I am heartily glad I came hither to you. If he comes to-morrow, I'll give him his payment. If ever he walks alone again, I'll never wrestle for prize more. And so God keep your worship.

OLIVER Farewell, good Charles. *[Exit* CHARLES*]*. Now will I stir this gamester. I hope I shall see an end of him; for my soul, yet I know not why, hates nothing more than he. Yet he's gentle, never schooled and yet learnèd, full of noble device, of all sorts enchantingly beloved. And indeed so much in the heart of the world, and especially of my own people, who best know him, that I am altogether despised. But it shall not be so long: this wrestler shall clear all. Nothing remains but that I kindle the boy thither, which now I'll go about.   *Exit.*

SCENE II
Before the Duke's Palace.

Enter ROSALIND *and* CELIA.

CELIA   I pray you, Rosalind, my sweet cousin, be merry.

ROSALIND   Dear Celia, I show more mirth that I am mistress of, and would you yet I were merrier? Unless you could teach me to forget a banished father, you must not teach me how to remember any extraordinary pleasure.

CELIA   Herein I see you love me not with the full weight that I love you. If my uncle, your banished father, had banished your uncle, the Duke my father, if you had been still with me, I could have taught my love to take your father for mine. So would you, if the truth of your love to me were so righteously tempered as mine is to you.

ROSALIND   Well, I will forget the condition of my state to rejoice in yours.

CELIA   You know my father has no child but I, and none is likely to have; and truly, when he dies, you shall be his heir; for what he has taken away from your father perforce, I will render you again in affection. By my honor, I will, and when I break that oath, let me turn monster. Therefore, my sweet Rose, my dear Rose, be merry.

ROSALIND   From henceforth I will, cousin, and devise sports. Let me see, what think you of falling in love?

CELIA   I pray do, to make sport; but love no man in good earnest, and no further in sport either than with safety of a pure blush you may in honor come off again.

ROSALIND   What shall be our sport then?

CELIA   Let us sit and mock the good housewife Fortune from her wheel, that her gifts may henceforth be bestowed equally.

ROSALIND   I would we could do so, for her benefits are mightily misplaced, and the bountiful blind woman does most mistake in her gifts to women.

CELIA   'Tis true, for those that she makes fair she scarce
makes honest, and those that she makes honest she
makes very ill-looking.

ROSALIND   Nay, now you go from Fortune's office to
Nature's. Fortune reigns in gifts of the world, not in the
lineaments of Nature.

Enter TOUCHSTONE, *the Clown.*

CELIA   No; when Nature has made a fair creature, may
she not by Fortune fall into the fire? Though Nature has
given us wit to flout at Fortune, has not Fortune sent in
this fool to cut off the argument?

ROSALIND   Indeed, there is Fortune too hard for Nature,
when Fortune makes Nature's natural the cutter-off of
Nature's wit.

CELIA   Perhaps this is not Fortune's work either, but
Nature's, which perceives our natural wits too dull to
reason of such goddesses and has sent this natural for our
whetstone. For always the dullness of the fool is the
whetstone of the wits. How now, wit; whither wander
you?

TOUCHSTONE   Mistress, you must come away to your
father.

CELIA   Were you made the messenger?

TOUCHSTONE   No, by my honor, but I was bid to come
for you.

ROSALIND   Where learned you that oath, fool?

TOUCHSTONE   Of a certain knight that swore by his
honor they were good pancakes, and swore by his honor
the mustard was naught. Now I'll stand to it, the pancakes were naught, and the mustard was good, and yet
was not the knight forsworn.

CELIA   How prove you that in the great heap of your
knowledge?

ROSALIND   Ay, now unmuzzle your wisdom.

TOUCHSTONE   Stand you both forth now. Stroke your
chins, and swear by your beards that I am a knave.

CELIA   By our beards, if we had them, you are.

TOUCHSTONE   By my knavery, if I had it, then I would be; but if you swear by that that is not, you are not forsworn. No more was this knight, swearing by his honor, for he never had any; or if he had, he had sworn it away before ever he saw those pancakes or that mustard.

CELIA   Pray, who is it that you mean?

TOUCHSTONE   One that old Frederick, your father, loves.

CELIA   My father's love is enough to honor him. Enough: speak no more of him; you'll be whipped for slander one of these days.

TOUCHSTONE   The more pity that fools may not speak wisely what wise men do foolishly.

CELIA   By my word, you say true, for since the little wit that fools have was silenced, the little foolery that wise men have makes a great show. Here comes Monsieur Le Beau.

Enter LE BEAU.

ROSALIND   With his mouth full of news.

CELIA   Which he will put on us as pigeons feed their young.

ROSALIND   Then shall we be news-crammed.

CELIA   All the better; we shall be the more marketable. Bon jour, Monsieur Le Beau, what's the news?

LE BEAU   Fair princess, you have lost much good sport.

CELIA   Sport; of what color?

LE BEAU   What color, madam? How shall I answer you?

ROSALIND   As wit and fortune will.

TOUCHSTONE   Or as the destinies decree.

CELIA   Well said; that was laid on with a trowel.

TOUCHSTONE   Nay, if I keep not my rank—

ROSALIND   You lose your old smell.

LE BEAU   You amaze me, ladies. I would have told you of good wrestling, which you have lost the sight of.

ROSALIND   Yet tell us the manner of the wrestling.

LE BEAU   I will tell you the beginning; and if it pleases
  your ladyships, you may see the end, for the best is yet to
  do. Here, where you are, they are coming to perform it.
CELIA   Well, the beginning that is dead and buried.
LE BEAU   There comes an old man with his three sons.
CELIA   I could match this beginning with an old tale.
LE BEAU   Three fine young men, of excellent growth and
  presence—
ROSALIND   With bills on their necks, 'Be it known unto
  all men by these presents.'
LE BEAU   The eldest of the three wrestled with Charles,
  the Duke's wrestler; which Charles in a moment threw
  him and broke three of his ribs, that there is little hope of
  life in him. So he served the second, and so the third.
  Yonder they lie, the poor old man, their father, making
  such pitiful dole over them that all the beholders take his
  part with weeping.
ROSALIND   Alas!
TOUCHSTONE   But what is the sport, monsieur, that the
  ladies have lost?
LE BEAU   Why, this that I speak of.
TOUCHSTONE   Thus men may grow wiser every day. It is
  the first time that ever I heard breaking of ribs was sport
  for ladies.
CELIA   Or I, I promise you.
ROSALIND   But is there any else longs to see this broken
  music in his sides? Is there yet another dotes upon rib-
  breaking? Shall we see this wrestling, cousin?
LE BEAU   You must, if you stay here, for here is the place
  appointed for the wrestling, and they are ready to
  perform it.
CELIA   Yonder sure they are coming. Let us now stay and
  see it.

Flourish. Enter DUKE FREDERICK, *Lords,* ORLANDO,
CHARLES, *and Attendants.*

DUKE FREDERICK   Come on. Since the youth will not be
  entreated, his own peril on his forwardness.

ROSALIND   Is yonder the man?

LE BEAU   Even he, madam.

CELIA   Alas, he is too young; yet he looks successfully.

DUKE FREDERICK   How now, daughter and cousin; are
  you crept hither to see the wrestling?

ROSALIND   Ay, my liege, so please you give us leave.

DUKE FREDERICK   You will take little delight in it, I can
  tell you, there is such odds in the man. In pity of the
  challenger's youth I would fain dissuade him, but he will
  not be entreated. Speak to him, ladies; see if you can
  move him.

CELIA   Call him hither, good Monsieur Le Beau.

DUKE FREDERICK   Do so. I'll not be by.

LE BEAU   Monsieur the challenger, the princess calls for
  you.

ORLANDO   I attend them with all respect and duty.

ROSALIND   Young man, have you challenged Charles the
  wrestler?

ORLANDO   No, fair princess. He is the general
  challenger; I come but in as others do, to try with him the
  strength of my youth.

CELIA   Young gentleman, your spirits are too bold for
  your years. You have seen cruel proof of this man's
  strength. If you saw yourself with your eyes or knew
  yourself with your judgment, the fear of your adventure
  would counsel you to a more equal enterprise. We pray
  you for your own sake to embrace your own safety and
  give over this attempt.

ROSALIND   Do, young sir. Your reputation shall not
  therefore be lost; we will make it our suit to the Duke
  that the wrestling might not go forward.

ORLANDO   I beseech you, punish me not with your hard
  thoughts, wherein I confess me much guilty to deny so
  fair and excellent ladies anything. But let your fair eyes
  and gentle wishes go with me to my trial; wherein if I am

thrown, there is but one shamed that was never gracious; if killed, but one dead that is willing to be so. I shall do my friends no wrong, for I have none to lament me; the world no injury, for in it I have nothing. Only in the world I fill up a place, which may be better supplied when I have made it empty.

ROSALIND   The little strength that I have, I would it were with you.

CELIA   And mine to eke out hers.

ROSALIND   Fare you well. Pray heaven I may be deceived in you!

CELIA   Your heart's desires be with you!

CHARLES   Come, where is this young gallant that is so desirous to lie with his mother earth?

ORLANDO   Ready, sir; but his will has in it a more modest working.

DUKE FREDERICK   You shall try but one fall.

CHARLES   No, I warrant your Grace you shall not entreat him to a second that have so mightily persuaded him from a first.

ORLANDO   You mean to mock me after. You should not have mocked me before. But come your ways.

ROSALIND   Now Hercules be your speed, young man!

CELIA   I would I were invisible, to catch the strong fellow by the leg.

[They wrestle.]

ROSALIND   O excellent young man!

CELIA   If I had a thunderbolt in my eye, I can tell who should down.

[Charles is thrown. Shout.]

DUKE FREDERICK   No more, no more.

ORLANDO   Yes, I beseech your Grace; I am not yet well breathed.

DUKE FREDERICK
    How do you, Charles?
LE BEAU   He cannot speak, my lord.
DUKE FREDERICK
    Bear him away.

                    [Charles is carried out.]

                    What is your name, young man?
ORLANDO   Orlando, my liege, the youngest son of Sir
    Rowland de Boys.
DUKE FREDERICK
    I would you had been son to some man else.
    The world esteemed your father honorable,
    But I did find him ever my enemy.
    You should have better pleased me with this deed
    Had you descended from another house.
    But fare you well; you are a gallant youth;
    I would you had told me of another father.
                                Exit Duke, with lords.

CELIA
    Were I my father, cousin, would I do this?
ORLANDO
    I am more proud to be Sir Rowland's son,
    His youngest son, and would not change that calling
    To be adopted heir to Frederick.
ROSALIND
    My father loved Sir Rowland as his soul,
    And all the world was of my father's mind.
    Had I before known this young man his son,
    I should have given him tears unto entreaties
    Ere he should thus have ventured.
CELIA   Gentle cousin,
    Let us go thank him and encourage him.
    My father's rough and envious disposition
    Sticks me at heart. Sir, you have well deserved;

If you do keep your promises in love
But justly as you have exceeded all promise,
Your mistress shall be happy.

ROSALIND   Gentleman,

[Gives him a chain from her neck.]

Wear this for me, one out of suits with fortune,
That could give more but that her hand lacks means.
Shall we go, cousin?

CELIA   Ay. Fare you well, fair gentleman.

ORLANDO

Can I not say 'I thank you'? My better parts
Are all thrown down, and that which here stands up
Is but a post, a mere lifeless block.

ROSALIND

He calls us back. My pride fell with my fortunes;
I'll ask him what he would. Did you call, sir?
Sir, you have wrestled well, and overthrown
More than your enemies.

CELIA   Will you go, cousin?

ROSALIND

Have with you. Fare you well.   *Exit with Celia.*

ORLANDO

What passion hangs these weights upon my tongue?
I cannot speak to her, yet she urged conference.

Enter LE BEAU.

O poor Orlando, you are overthrown!
Or Charles or something weaker masters you.

LE BEAU

Good sir, I do in friendship counsel you
To leave this place. Albeit you have deserved
High commendation, true applause, and love,
Yet such is now the Duke's condition
He misinterprets all that you have done.

The Duke is changeable. What he is, indeed,
More suits you to conceive than I to speak of.

ORLANDO

I thank you, sir; and pray you tell me this:
Which of the two was daughter of the Duke,
That here was at the wrestling?

LE BEAU

Neither his daughter, if we judge by manners,
But yet indeed the smaller is his daughter,
The other is daughter to the banished Duke,
And here detained by her usurping uncle
To keep his daughter company, whose loves
Are dearer than the natural bond of sisters.
But I can tell you that of late this Duke
Has taken displeasure at his gentle niece,
Grounded upon no other argument
But that the people praise her for her virtues
And pity her for her good father's sake.
And, on my life, his malice against the lady
Will suddenly break forth. Sir, fare you well.
Hereafter, in a better world than this,
I shall desire more love and knowledge of you.

ORLANDO

I rest much bounden to you. Fare you well.

Exit Le Beau.

Thus must I from the smoke into the smother,
From tyrant Duke unto a tyrant brother,
But heavenly Rosalind!   *Exit.*

SCENE III

A room in the Palace.

Enter CELIA *and* ROSALIND.

CELIA   Why, cousin, why, Rosalind! Cupid have mercy,
not a word?

ROSALIND   Not one to throw at a dog.

CELIA   No, your words are too precious to be cast away
   upon curs; throw some of them at me; come, lame me
   with reasons.

ROSALIND   Then there were two cousins laid up, when
   the one should be lamed with reasons and the other mad
   without any.

CELIA   But is all this for your father?

ROSALIND   No, some of it is for my child's father. O, how
   full of briers is this working-day world!

CELIA   They are but burrs, cousin, thrown upon you in
   holiday foolery; if we walk not in the trodden paths, our
   very petticoats will catch them.

ROSALIND   I could shake them off my coat; these burrs
   are in my heart.

CELIA   Hem them away.

ROSALIND   I would try, if I could cry 'hem,' and have
   him.

CELIA   Come, come, wrestle with your affections.

ROSALIND   O, they take the part of a better wrestler than
   myself!

CELIA   O, a good wish upon you! You will cry in time, in
   despite of a fall. But turning these jests out of service, let
   us talk in good earnest. Is it possible on such a sudden
   you should fall into so strong a liking with old Sir
   Rowland's youngest son?

ROSALIND   The Duke my father loved his father dearly.

CELIA   Does it therefore ensue that you should love his
   son dearly? By this kind of chase, I should hate him, for
   my father hated his father dearly; yet I hate not Orlando.

ROSALIND   No, faith, hate him not, for my sake.

CELIA   Why should I not? Does he not deserve well?

Enter DUKE FREDERICK, *with Lords.*

ROSALIND   Let me love him for that, and do you love him
   because I do. Look, here comes the Duke.

CELIA   With his eyes full of anger.

DUKE FREDERICK
   Mistress, dispatch you with your safest haste
   And get you from our court.

ROSALIND   Me, uncle?

DUKE FREDERICK   You, niece.
   Within these ten days if you should be found
   So near our public court as twenty miles,
   You die for it.

ROSALIND   I do beseech your Grace
   Let me the knowledge of my fault bear with me.
   If with myself I hold intelligence
   Or have acquaintance with my own desires,
   If I do not dream or am not frantic,
   As I do trust I am not; then, dear uncle,
   Never so much as in a thought unborn
   Did I offend your Highness.

DUKE FREDERICK   Thus do all traitors.
   If their purgation did consist in words,
   They are as innocent as grace itself.
   Let it suffice you that I trust you not.

ROSALIND
   Yet your mistrust cannot make me a traitor.
   Tell me whereon the likelihood depends.

DUKE FREDERICK
   You are your father's daughter, there's enough.

ROSALIND
   So was I when your Highness took his dukedom;
   So was I when your Highness banished him.
   Treason is not inherited, my lord,
   Or if we did derive it from our friends,
   What's that to me? My father was no traitor.
   Then, good my liege, mistake me not so much
   To think my poverty is treacherous.

CELIA
   Dear sovereign, hear me speak.

DUKE FREDERICK
   Ay, Celia. We stayed her for your sake,
   Else had she with her father ranged along.

CELIA

  I did not then entreat to have her stay;
  It was your pleasure and your own remorse.
  I was too young that time to value her,
  But now I know her. If she is a traitor,
  Why, so am I. We ever have slept together,
  Rose at an instant, learned, played, ate
    together;
  And wheresoever we went, like Juno's swans,
  Always we went coupled and inseparable.

DUKE FREDERICK

  She is too subtle for you; and her smoothness,
  Her very silence and her patience,
  Speak to the people, and they pity her.
  You are a fool. She robs you of your name,
  And you will show more bright and seem more
    virtuous
  When she is gone. Then open not your lips.
  Firm and irrevocable is my word
  Which I have passed upon her; she is banished.

CELIA

  Pronounce that sentence then on me, my liege;
  I cannot live out of her company.

DUKE FREDERICK

  You are a fool. You, niece, provide yourself;
  If you outstay the time, upon my honor,
  And in the greatness of my word, you die.

                        Exeunt Duke and Lords.

CELIA

  O my poor Rosalind, whither will you go?
  Will you change fathers? I will give you mine.
  I charge you be not you more grieved than I am.

ROSALIND

  I have more cause.

CELIA   You have not, cousin.
  Pray, be cheerful. Know you not the Duke
  Has banished me, his daughter?

ROSALIND   That he has not.

CELIA

No? has not? Rosalind lacks then the love
Which teaches you that you and I are one.
Shall we be sundered, shall we part, sweet girl?
No, let my father seek another heir.
Therefore advise with me how we may fly,
Whither to go, and what to bear with us.
And do not seek to take your change upon you,
To bear your griefs yourself and leave me out;
For, by this heaven, now at our sorrows' edge,
Say what you can, I'll go along with you.

ROSALIND

Why, whither shall we go?

CELIA

To seek my uncle in the Forest of Arden.

ROSALIND

Alas, what danger will it be to us,
Maids as we are, to travel forth so far!
Beauty provokes thieves sooner than gold.

CELIA

I'll put myself in poor and mean attire
And with a kind of umber smirch my face;
The like do you; so shall we pass along
And never stir assailants.

ROSALIND   Were it not better,
Because now I am more than common tall,
That I did suit me all points like a man?
A gallant rapier upon my thigh,
A boar-spear in my hand; and, in my heart
Lie there what hidden woman's fear there will,
We'll have a swashing and a martial outside
As many other mannish cowards have
That do outface it with their semblances.

CELIA

What shall I call you when you are a man?

ROSALIND

I'll have no worse a name than Jove's own page,
and therefore look you call me Ganymede.
But what will you be called?

CELIA

Something that has a reference to my state:
No longer Celia, but Aliena.

ROSALIND

But, cousin, what if we essayed to steal
The clownish fool out of your father's court
Would he not be a comfort to our travel?

CELIA

He'll go along o'er the wide world with me;
Leave me alone to woo him. Let's away
And get our jewels and our wealth together,
Devise the fittest time and safest way
To hide us from pursuit that will be made
After my flight. Now go we in content
To liberty, and not to banishment.   *Exeunt.*

Act II

✿

SCENE I
The Forest of Arden.

Enter DUKE SENIOR, AMIENS, *and two or three Lords.*

DUKE SENIOR
  Now, my co-mates and brothers in exile,
  Has not old custom made this life more sweet
  Than that of painted pomp? Are not these woods
  More free from peril than the envious court?
  Here feel we not the penalty of Adam,
  The seasons' difference, as the icy fang
  And churlish chiding of the winter's wind,
  Which, when it bites and blows upon my body
  Even till I shrink with cold, I smile and say
  'This is no flattery'. These are counsellors
  That feelingly persuade me what I am.
  Sweet are the uses of adversity,
  Which, like the toad, ugly and venomous,
  Wears yet a precious jewel in its head.
  And this our life, exempt from public haunt,
  Finds tongues in trees, books in the running brooks,
  Sermons in stones, and good in everything.
AMIENS
  I would not change it. Happy is your Grace
  That can translate the stubbornness of fortune
  Into so quiet and so sweet a style.
DUKE SENIOR
  Come, shall we go and kill us venison?
  And yet it irks me the poor dappled fools,

Being native burghers of this desert city,
 Should, in their own confines, with forkèd heads
 Have their round haunches gored.
FIRST LORD   Indeed, my lord,
 The melancholy Jaques grieves at that,
 And in that kind swears you do more usurp
 Than does your brother that has banished you.
 To-day my Lord of Amiens and myself
 Did steal behind him as he lay along
 Under an oak, whose antique root peeps out
 Upon the brook that brawls along this wood.
 To which place a poor sequestered stag
 That from the hunter's aim had taken a hurt
 Did come to languish. And indeed, my lord,
 The wretched animal heaved forth such groans
 That their discharge did stretch his leathern coat
 Almost to bursting, and the big round tears
 Coursed one another down his innocent nose
 In piteous chase. And thus the hairy fool,
 Much markèd of the melancholy Jaques,
 Stood on the extremest verge of the swift brook,
 Augmenting it with tears.
DUKE SENIOR   But what said Jaques?
 Did he not moralize this spectacle?
FIRST LORD
 O, yes, into a thousand similes.
 First, for his weeping into the needless stream:
 'Poor deer,' said he, 'you make a testament
 As worldlings do, giving your sum of more
 To that which had too much.' Then, being there alone,
 Left and abandoned of his velvet friend:
 'Tis right,' said he, 'thus misery does part
 The flux of company.' Anon a careless herd,
 Full of the pasture, jumps along by him
 And never stays to greet him. 'Ay,' said Jaques,

'Sweep on, you fat and greasy citizens,
'Tis just the fashion; wherefore do you look
Upon that poor and broken bankrupt there?'
Thus most invectively he pierces through
The body of the country, city, court,
Yea, and of this our life; swearing that we
Are mere usurpers, tyrants, and what's worse,
To fright the animals and to kill them up
In their assigned and native dwelling place.

DUKE SENIOR
And did you leave him in this contemplation?

SECOND LORD
We did, my lord, weeping and commenting
Upon the sobbing deer.

DUKE SENIOR   Show me the place.
I love to catch him in these sullen fits,
For then he's full of matter.

FIRST LORD
I'll bring you to him straight   *Exeunt.*

SCENE II
A room in the Palace.

Enter DUKE FREDERICK, *with Lords.*

DUKE FREDERICK
Can it be possible that no man saw them?
It cannot be; some villains of my court
Are of consent and sufferance in this.

FIRST LORD
I cannot hear of any that did see her.
The ladies her attendants of her chamber
Saw her abed, and in the morning early
They found the bed untreasured of their mistress.

SECOND LORD
My lord, the scurvy clown at whom so oft
Your Grace was wont to laugh is also missing.
Hisperia, the princess' gentlewoman,

Confesses that she secretly overheard
Your daughter and her cousin much commend
The parts and graces of the wrestler
That did but lately throw the sinewy Charles.
And she believes, wherever they are gone,
That youth is surely in their company.

DUKE FREDERICK
Send to his brother, fetch that gallant hither;
If he is absent, bring his brother to me;
I'll make him find him. Do this suddenly,
And let not search and inquisition quail
To bring again these foolish runaways.   *Exeunt.*

SCENE III
Before Oliver's house.

Enter ORLANDO *and* ADAM.

ORLANDO
Who's there?

ADAM
What, my young master, O my gentle master,
O my sweet master, O you memory
Of old Sir Rowland, why, what make you here?
Why are you virtuous? Why do people love you?
And wherefore are you gentle, strong, and valiant?
Why would you be so willing to overcome
The bonny prizer of the changeable Duke?
Your praise is come too swiftly home before you.
Know you not, master, to some kind of men
Their graces serve them but as enemies?
And so do yours. Your virtues, gentle master,
Are sanctified and holy traitors to you.
O, what a world is this, when what is comely
Envenoms him that bears it!

ORLANDO
Why, what's the matter?

ADAM   O unhappy youth,

Come not within these doors; within this roof
The enemy of all your graces lives.
Your brother, no, no brother, yet the son—
Yet not the son, I will not call him son—
Of him I was about to call his father,
Has heard your praises, and this night he means
To burn the lodging where you use to lie
And you within it. If he fails of that,
He will have other means to cut you off.
I overheard him, and his practices;
This is no place, this house is but a butchery;
Abhor it, fear it, do not enter it!

ORLANDO

Why, whither, Adam, would you have me go?

ADAM

No matter whither, so you come not here.

ORLANDO

What, would you have me go and beg my food,
Or with a base and boisterous sword enforce
A thievish living on the common road?
This I must do, or know not what to do;
Yet this I will not do, do how I can.
I rather will subject me to the malice
Of a diverted blood and bloody brother.

ADAM

But do not so. I have five hundred crowns,
The thrifty hire I saved under your father,
Which I did store to be my foster nurse
When service should in my old limbs lie lame
And unregarded age in corners thrown.
Take that, and he that does the ravens feed,
Yea, providently caters for the sparrow,
Be comfort to my age. Here is the gold,
All this I give you. Let me be your servant;
Though I look old, yet I am strong and lusty,
For in my youth I never did apply
Hot and rebellious liquors in my blood;
Nor did I with unbashful forehead woo

The means of weakness and debility.
Therefore my age is as a lusty winter,
Frosty, but kindly. Let me go with you;
I'll do the service of a younger man
In all your business and necessities.

ORLANDO

O good old man, how well in you appears
The constant service of the antique world,
When service sweat for duty, not reward!
You are not for the fashion of these times,
Where none will sweat but for promotiòn,
And having that, do choke their service up
Even with the having; it is not so with you.
But, poor old man, you prune a rotten tree
That cannot so much as a blossom yield
In lieu of all your pains and husbandry.
But come your ways, we'll go along together,
And ere we have your youthful wages spent,
We'll light upon some settled low content.

ADAM

Master, go on, and I will follow you
To the last gasp with truth and loyalty.
From seventeen years till now almost fourscore
Here livèd I, but now live here no more;
At seventeen years many their fortunes seek,
But at fourscore it is too late a week.
Yet fortune cannot recompense me better
Than to die well and not my master's debtor.   *Exeunt.*

SCENE IV
The Forest of Arden.

Enter ROSALIND *as Ganymede,* CELIA *as Aliena,*
and TOUCHSTONE.

ROSALIND   O Jupiter, how weary are my spirits!

TOUCHSTONE I care not for my spirits if my legs were not weary.

ROSALIND I could find in my heart to disgrace my man's apparel and to cry like a woman; but I must comfort the weaker vessel, as doublet and hose ought to show itself courageous to petticoat. Therefore, courage, good Aliena!

CELIA I pray you bear with me; I can go no further.

TOUCHSTONE For my part, I had rather bear with you than bear you; yet I should bear no cross if I did bear you; for I think you have no money in your purse.

ROSALIND Well, this is the Forest of Arden.

TOUCHSTONE Ay, now am I in Arden, the more fool I. When I was at home, I was in a better place, but travellers must be content.

Enter CORIN *and* SILVIUS.

ROSALIND

Ay, be so, good Touchstone. Look you, who come here,
A young man and an old in solemn talk.

CORIN

That is the way to make her scorn you ever.

SILVIUS

O Corin, that you knew how I do love her!

CORIN

I partly guess, for I have loved ere now.

SILVIUS

No, Corin, being old, you can not guess,
Though in your youth you were as true a lover
As ever sighed upon a midnight pillow.
But if your love were ever like to mine,
As sure I think did never man love so,
How many actions most ridiculous
Have you been drawn to by your fantasy?

CORIN

Into a thousand that I have forgotten.

SILVIUS

O, you did then never love so heartily!
If you remember not the slightest folly

That ever love did make you run into,
You have not loved.
Or if you have not sat as I do now,
Wearying your hearer in your mistress' praise,
You have not loved.
Or if you have not broken from company
Abruptly, as my passion now makes me,
You have not loved. O Phebe, Phebe, Phebe!   *Exit.*

ROSALIND

Alas, poor shepherd! Searching of your wound,
I have by hard adventure found my own.

TOUCHSTONE   And I mine. I remember, when I was in love
I broke my sword upon a stone and bid him take that for
coming a-night to Jane Smile. And I remember the
kissing of her scrubbing-brush, and the cow's teats that
her pretty chapped hands had milked. And I remember
the wooing of a peascod instead of her, from whom I took
two cods, and giving her them again, said with weeping
tears, 'Wear these for my sake.' We that are true lovers run
into strange capers; but as all is mortal in nature, so is all
nature in love mortal in folly.

ROSALIND   You speak wiser than you are aware of.

TOUCHSTONE   Nay, I shall never be aware of my own wit
till I break my shins against it.

ROSALIND

Jove, Jove! this shepherd's passion
Is much upon my fashion.

TOUCHSTONE

And mine, but it grows something stale with me.

CELIA

I pray you, one of you question yon man
If he for gold will give us any food.
I faint almost to death.

TOUCHSTONE   Holla, you clown!

ROSALIND

Peace, fool! he's not your kinsman.

CORIN

Who calls?

TOUCHSTONE   Your betters, sir.

CORIN   Else are they very wretched.

ROSALIND

Peace, I say! Good even to you, friend.

CORIN

And to you, gentle sir, and to you all.

ROSALIND

I pray you, shepherd, if perhaps love or gold
Can in this desert place buy entertainment,
Bring us where we may rest ourselves and feed.
Here's a young maid with travel much oppressed,
And faints for succor.

CORIN   Fair sir, I pity her
And wish, for her sake more than for my own,
My fortunes were more able to relieve her;
But I am shepherd to another man
And do not shear the fleeces that I graze.
My master is of churlish disposition
And little recks to find the way to heaven
By doing deeds of hospitality.
Besides, his cottage, flocks, and bounds of feed
Are now on sale, and at our sheepcote now,
By reason of his absence, there is nothing
That you will feed on; but what is, come see,
And in my voice most welcome shall you be.

ROSALIND

What is he that shall buy his flock and pasture?

CORIN

That young swain that you saw here but erewhile,
That little cares for buying anything.

ROSALIND

I pray you, if it stands with honesty,
Buy you the cottage, pasture, and the flock,
And you shall have to pay for it of us.

CELIA

And we will mend your wages. I like this place
And willingly could waste my time in it.

CORIN

Assuredly the thing is to be sold.

Go with me; if you like upon report
The soil, the profit, and this kind of life,
I will your very faithful feeder be
And buy it with your gold right suddenly.   *Exeunt.*

SCENE V
Another part of the Forest.

Enter AMIENS, JAQUES, *and others.*

Song.

AMIENS   Under the greenwood tree
              Who loves to lie with me,
          And turn his merry note
              Unto the sweet bird's throat,
          Come hither, come hither, come hither.
              Here shall he see no enemy
          But winter and rough weather.

JAQUES   More, more, I pray you more!

AMIENS   It will make you melancholy, Monsieur Jaques.

JAQUES   I thank it. More, I pray you more! I can suck
    melancholy out of a song as a weasel sucks eggs. More,
    I pray more!

AMIENS   My voice is ragged. I know I cannot please you.

JAQUES   I do not desire you to please me; I desire you to
    sing. Come, more, another stanza! Call you them
    stanzas?

AMIENS   What you will, Monsieur Jaques.

JAQUES   Nay, I care not for their names; they owe me
    nothing. Will you sing?

AMIENS   More at your request than to please myself.

JAQUES   Well then, if ever I thank any man, I'll thank
    you. But that they call compliment is like the encounter
    of two dog-apes, and when a man thanks me heartily, I
    think I have given him a penny and he renders me the

beggarly thanks. Come, sing; and you that will not, hold
your tongues.

AMIENS   Well, I'll end the song. Sirs, set the table; the
Duke will drink under this tree. He has been all this day
to look for you.

JAQUES   And I have been all this day to avoid him. He is
too disputable for my company. I think of as many
matters as he, but I give heaven thanks and make no
boast of them. Come, warble, come.

Song.
All sing.

Who does ambition shun
    And loves to live in the sun,
Seeking the food he eats,
    And pleased with what he gets,
Come hither, come hither, come hither.
    Here shall he see no enemy
    But winter and rough weather.

JAQUES   I'll give you a verse to this note that I made
yesterday in despite of my invention.

AMIENS   And I'll sing it.

JAQUES   Thus it goes.

[Gives a paper.]

AMIENS   If it does come to pass
        That any man turn ass,
        Leaving his wealth and ease
        A stubborn will to please,
        Ducdame, ducdame, ducdame.[1]
        Here shall he see gross fools as he,
        If he will come to me.

---

[1]Come with me (from Welsh).

What's that 'ducdame'?

JAQUES 'Tis a Greek invocation to call fools into a circle. I'll go sleep, if I can; if I cannot, I'll rail against all the first-born of Egypt.

AMIENS And I'll go seek the Duke. His banquet is prepared. *Exeunt.*

SCENE VI
Another part of the Forest.

Enter ORLANDO *and* ADAM.

ADAM Dear master, I can go no further. O, I die for food. Here lie I down and measure out my grave. Farewell, kind master.

ORLANDO Why, how now, Adam? no greater heart in you? Live a little, comfort a little, cheer yourself a little. If this uncouth forest yields anything savage, I will either be food for it or bring it for food to you. Your fancy is nearer death than your powers. For my sake be comfortable; hold death awhile at the arm's end. I will here be with you presently, and if I bring you not something to eat, I will give you leave to die; but if you die before I come, you are a mocker of my labor. Well said; you look cheerily, and I'll be with you quickly. Yet you lie in the bleak air. Come, I will bear you to some shelter, and you shall not die for lack of a dinner if there lives anything in this desert. Cheerily, good Adam. *Exeunt.*

SCENE 7
Another part of the Forest.

Enter DUKE SENIOR, *and Lords.*

DUKE SENIOR
I think he is transformed into a beast,
For I can nowhere find him like a man.

FIRST LORD
  My lord, he is but even now gone hence;
  Here was he merry, hearing of a song.

DUKE SENIOR
  If he, compact of jars, grows musical,
  We shall have shortly discord in the spheres.
  Go seek him; tell him I would speak with him.

Enter JAQUES.

FIRST LORD
  He saves my labor by his own approach.

DUKE SENIOR
  Why, how now, monsieur, what a life is this,
  That your poor friends must woo your company?
  What, you look merrily.

JAQUES
  A fool, a fool! I met a fool in the forest,
  A motley fool! a miserable world!
  As I do live by food, I met a fool
  Who laid him down and basked him in the sun
  And railed on Lady Fortune in good terms,
  In good set terms, and yet a motley fool.
  'Good morrow, fool,' said I. 'No, sir,' said he,
  'Call me not fool till heaven has sent me fortune.'
  And then he drew a dial from his pocket,
  And looking on it with lack-lustre eye,
  Says very wisely, 'It is ten o'clock.
  Thus we may see,' said he, 'how the world wags.
  'Tis but an hour ago since it was nine,
  And after one hour more it will be eleven;
  And so, from hour to hour, we ripe and ripe,
  And then, from hour to hour, we rot and rot;
  And thereby hangs a tale.' When I did hear
  The motley fool thus moral on the time,
  My lungs began to crow like chanticleer
  That fools should be so deep contemplative;
  And I did laugh without intermission

An hour by his dial. O noble fool,
A worthy fool! Motley's the only wear.

DUKE SENIOR
What fool is this?

JAQUES
O worthy fool! One that has been a courtier,
And says, if ladies are but young and fair,
They have the gift to know it. And in his brain,
Which is as dry as the remainder biscuit
After a voyage, he has strange places crammed
With observation, which he then vents
In mangled forms. O that I were a fool!
I am ambitious for a motley coat.

DUKE SENIOR
You shall have one.

JAQUES   It is my only suit,
Provided that you weed your better judgments
Of all opinion that grows rank in them
That I am wise. I must have liberty
With it, as large a charter as the wind,
To blow on whom I please, for so fools have.
And they that are most gallèd with my folly,
They most must laugh. And why, sir, must they so?
The why is plain as way to parish church:
He that a fool does very wisely hit
Does very foolishly, although he smarts
Within, seems senseless of the joke. If not,
The wise man's folly is anatomized
Even by the squandering glances of the fool.
Invest me in my motley, give me leave
To speak my mind, and I will through and through
Cleanse the foul body of the infected world,
If they will patiently receive my medicine.

DUKE SENIOR
Fie on you! I can tell what you would do.

JAQUES
What, for a counter, would I do but good?

DUKE SENIOR
Most mischievous foul sin, in chiding sin.

For you yourself have been a libertine,
As sensual as the brutish sting itself.
And all the swollen sores and headed evils
That you with license of free foot have caught,
Would you disgorge into the general world.

JAQUES

Why, who cries out on pride
That can therein tax any private party?
Does it not flow as hugely as the sea
Till then the weary very means do ebb?
What woman in the city do I name
When I do say the city woman bears
The cost of princes on unworthy shoulders?
Who can come in and say that I mean her,
When such a one as she, such is her neighbor?
Or what is he of basest function
That says his bravery is not at my cost,
Thinking that I mean him, but therein suits
His folly to the mettle of my speech?
There then, how then, what then? Let me see wherein
My tongue has wronged him. If it does him right,
Then he has wronged himself. If he is free,
Why, then my taxing like a wild goose flies
Unclaimed of any man. But who comes here?

Enter ORLANDO.

ORLANDO

Forbear, and eat no more!
JAQUES   Why, I have eaten none yet.
ORLANDO

Nor shall you, till necessity be served.
JAQUES

Of what kind should this cock come of?
DUKE SENIOR

Are you thus boldened, man, by your distress,
Or else a rude despiser of good manners,
That in civility you seem so empty?

ORLANDO

    You touched my vein at first. The thorny point
    Of bare distress has taken from me the show
    Of smooth civility; yet am I better bred
    And know some nurture. But forbear, I say!
    He dies that touches any of this fruit
    Till I and my affairs are answerèd.

JAQUES

    If you will not be answered with reason, I must die.

DUKE SENIOR

    What would you have? Your gentleness shall force
    More than your force move us to gentleness.

ORLANDO

    I almost die for food, and let me have it!

DUKE SENIOR

    Sit down and feed, and welcome to our table.

ORLANDO

    Speak you so gently? Pardon me, I pray you.
    I thought that all things had been savage here,
    And therefore put I on the countenance
    Of stern commandment. But whatever you are
    That in this desert inaccessible,
    Under the shade of melancholy boughs,
    Lose and neglect the creeping hours of time;
    If ever you have looked on better days,
    If ever been where bells have knolled to church,
    If ever sat at any good man's feast,
    If ever from your eyelids wiped a tear
    And know what 'tis to pity and be pitied,
    Let gentleness my strong enforcement be;
    In which hope now I blush, and hide my sword.

DUKE SENIOR

    True is it that we have seen better days,
    And have with holy bell been knolled to church,
    And sat at good men's feasts, and wiped our eyes
    Of drops that sacred pity has engendered.
    And therefore sit you down in gentleness,
    And take upon command what help we have
    That to your wanting may be ministered.

ORLANDO
> Then but forbear your food a little while,
> While, like a doe, I go to find my fawn
> And give it food. There is an old poor man
> Who after me has many a weary step
> Limped in pure love. Till he is first sufficed,
> Oppressed with two weak evils, age and hunger,
> I will not touch a bit.

DUKE SENIOR   Go find him out,
> And we will nothing waste till you return.

ORLANDO
> I thank you, and be blest for your good comfort!

> *[Exit.]*

DUKE SENIOR
> You see we are not all alone unhappy:
> This wide and universal theatre
> Presents more woeful pageants than the scene
> Wherein we play.

JAQUES   All the world's a stage,
> And all the men and women merely players;
> They have their exits and their entrances,
> And one man in his time plays many parts,
> His acts being seven ages. At first, the infant,
> Mewling and puking in the nurse's arms.
> Then the whining schoolboy, with his satchel
> And shining morning face, creeping like snail
> Unwillingly to school. And then the lover,
> Sighing like furnace, with a woeful ballad
> Made to his mistress' eyebrow. Then a soldier,
> Full of strange oaths and bearded like the leopard,
> Jealous in honor, sudden and quick in quarrel,
> Seeking the bubble reputation
> Even in the cannon's mouth. And then the justice,
> In fair round belly with good capon lined,
> With eyes severe and beard of formal cut,
> Full of wise sayings and usual instances;
> And so he plays his part. The sixth age shifts

Into the lean and slippered pantaloon,
With spectacles on nose and pouch on side;
His youthful hose, well saved, a world too wide
For his shrunk shank; and his big manly voice,
Turning again toward childish treble, pipes
And whistles in his sound. Last scene of all,
That ends this strange eventful history,
Is second childishness and mere oblivion,
No teeth, no eyes, no taste, no anything.

Enter ORLANDO, *with* ADAM.

DUKE SENIOR
Welcome. Set down your venerable burden
And let him feed.
ORLANDO
I thank you most for him.
ADAM   So had you need.
I scarce can speak to thank you for myself.
DUKE SENIOR
Welcome, fall to. I will not trouble you
As yet to question you about your fortunes.
Give us some music; and, good cousin, sing.

Song.

AMIENS   Blow, blow, you winter wind,
                You are not so unkind
                    As man's ingratitude:
                Your tooth is not so keen,
                Because you are not seen,
                    Although your breath is rude.
            Heigh-ho, sing heigh-ho, unto the green holly.
            Most friendship is wishing, most loving mere
                folly:
                    Then, heigh-ho, the holly.
                    This life is most jolly.

Freeze, freeze, you bitter sky
That does not bite so nigh
As benefits forgot:
Though you the waters warp,
Your sting is not so sharp
As friend remembered not.
Heigh-ho, sing, &c.

DUKE SENIOR
If then you were the good Sir Rowland's son,
As you have whispered faithfully you were,
And as my eye does his resemblance witness
Most truly limned and living in your face,
Be truly welcome hither. I am the Duke
That loved your father. The residue of your fortune
Go to my cave and tell me. Good old man,
You are right welcome, as your master is.
Support him by the arm. Give me your hand,
And let me all your fortunes understand.   *Exeunt.*

Act III

SCENE I
A room in the Palace.

Enter DUKE FREDERICK, LORDS, *and* OLIVER.

DUKE FREDERICK
Not see him since? Sir, sir, that cannot be.
But were I not the better part made mercy,
I should not seek an absent argument
Of my revenge, you present. But look to it:
Find out your brother, wheresoever he is.
Seek him with candle; bring him dead or living
Within this twelvemonth, or return no more
To seek a living in our territory.
Your lands, and all things that you do call yours
Worth seizure, do we seize into our hands
Till you can quit you by your brother's mouth
Of what we think against you.

OLIVER
O that your Highness knew my heart in this!
I never loved my brother in my life.

DUKE FREDERICK
More villain you. Well, push him out of doors,
And let my officers of such a nature
Make a seizure of his house and lands.
Do this immediately and turn him going.   *Exeunt.*

SCENE II
The Forest of Arden.

Enter ORLANDO, *with a paper.*

ORLANDO
Hang there, my verse, in witness of my love;
And you, thrice-crownèd Queen of night, survey
With your chaste eye, from your pale sphere above,
    Your huntress' name that my full life does sway.
O Rosalind! these trees shall be my books,
    And in their barks my thoughts I'll character,
That every eye which in this forest looks
    Shall see your virtue witnessed everywhere.
Run, run, Orlando, carve on every tree
The fair, the chaste, and inexpressible she.   *Exit.*

Enter CORIN *and* TOUCHSTONE.

CORIN   And how like you this shepherd's life, Master
Touchstone?

TOUCHSTONE   Truly, shepherd, in respect of itself, it is a
good life; but in respect that it is a shepherd's life, it is
naught. In respect that it is solitary, I like it very well; but
in respect that it is private, it is a very vile life. Now in
respect it is in the fields, it pleases me well; but in respect
it is not in the court, it is tedious. As it is a spare life, look
you, it fits my humor well; but as there is no more plenty
in it, it goes much against my stomach. Any philosophy
in you, shepherd?

CORIN   No more but that I know the more one sickens
the worse at ease he is; and that he that wants money,
means, and content is without three good friends. That
the property of rain is to wet and fire to burn; that good
pasture makes fat sheep, and that a great cause of the
night is lack of the sun. That he that has learned no wit
by nature nor art may complain of good breeding, or
comes of a very dull kindred.

TOUCHSTONE   Such a one is a natural philosopher. Were
you ever in court, shepherd?

CORIN   No, truly.

TOUCHSTONE   Then you are damned.

CORIN   Nay, I hope.

TOUCHSTONE   Truly you are damned, like an ill-roasted
egg, all on one side.

CORIN   For not being at court? Your reason.

TOUCHSTONE   Why, if you never were at court, you never
saw good manners, if you never saw good manners,
then your masters must be wicked; and wickedness is
sin, and sin is damnation. You are in a parlous state,
shepherd.

CORIN   Not a whit, Touchstone. Those that are good
manners at the court are as ridiculous in the country as
the behavior of the country is most mockable at the
court. You told me you salute not at the court, but you
kiss your hands. That courtesy would be uncleanly if
courtiers were shepherds.

TOUCHSTONE   Instance, briefly; come, instance.

CORIN   Why, we are ever handling our ewes, and their
fleeces you know are greasy.

TOUCHSTONE   Why, do not your courtier's hands
sweat? and is not the grease of a mutton as wholesome as
the sweat of a man? Shallow, shallow. A better instance,
I say; come.

CORIN   Besides, our hands are hard.

TOUCHSTONE   Your lips will feel them the sooner.
Shallow again. A more sound instance, come.

CORIN   And they are often tarred over with the surgery
of our sheep, and would you have us kiss tar? The courtier's hands are perfumed with civet.

TOUCHSTONE   Most shallow man! You worms' meat in
respect of a good piece of flesh indeed! Learn of the wise,
and consider. Civet is of a baser birth than tar, the very
uncleanly flux of a cat. Mend the instance, shepherd.

CORIN   You have too courtly a wit for me; I'll rest.

TOUCHSTONE   Will you rest damned? God help you,

shallow man! God make incision in you! you are raw.

CORIN   Sir, I am a true laborer; I earn that I eat, get
that I wear, owe no man hate, envy no man's happiness,
glad of other men's good, content with my harm; and the
greatest of my pride is to see my ewes graze and my lambs
suck.

TOUCHSTONE   That is another simple sin in you: to
bring the ewes and the rams together and to offer to get
your living by the copulation of cattle: to be bawd to a
bellwether and to betray a she-lamb of a twelvemonth to
a crookèd-pated old cuckoldly ram, out of all reasonable
match. If you are not damned for this, the devil himself
will have no shepherds; I cannot see else how you should
escape.

CORIN   Here comes young Master Ganymede, my new
mistress's brother.

Enter ROSALIND, *with a paper.*

ROSALIND   *[reads]*
         'From the east to western Ind,
         No jewel is like Rosalind.
         Her worth, being mounted on the wind,
         Through all the world bears Rosalind.
         All the pictures fairest lined
         Are but black to Rosalind.
         Let no face be kept in mind
         But the fair of Rosalind.'

TOUCHSTONE   I'll rhyme you so eight years together,
dinners and suppers and sleeping hours excepted. It is the
right butterwomen's jog to market.

ROSALIND   Out fool!

TOUCHSTONE   For a taste:
         If a hart does lack a hind,
         Let him seek out Rosalind.
         If the cat will after kind,
         So be sure will Rosalind.
         Winter garments must be lined,

So must slender Rosalind.
They that reap must sheaf and bind,
Then to cart with Rosalind.
Sweetest nut has sourest rind,
Such a nut is Rosalind.
He that sweetest rose will find
Must find love's prick, and Rosalind.

This is the very false gallop of verses. Why do you infect
yourself with them?

ROSALIND   Peace, you dull fool! I found them on a tree.

TOUCHSTONE   Truly the tree yields bad fruit.

ROSALIND   I'll graft it with you and then I shall graft it
with a medlar. Then it will be the earliest fruit in the
country; for you'll be rotten ere you are half ripe, and
that's the right virtue of the medlar.

TOUCHSTONE   You have said; but whether wisely or no,
let the forest judge.

Enter CELIA, *with a paper.*

ROSALIND   Peace! Here comes my sister reading; stand
aside.

CELIA   'Why should this a desert be?
       For it is unpeopled? No.
Tongues I'll hang on every tree
       That shall civil sayings show:
Some, how brief the life of man
       Runs his erring pilgrimage,
That the stretching of a span
       Buckles in his sum of age;
Some, of violated vows
       'Tween the souls of friend and friend.
But upon the fairest boughs,
       Or at every sentence end,
Will I "Rosalinda" write,
       Teaching all that read to know
The quintessence of every sprite
       Heaven would in little show.

Therefore heaven Nature charged
 That one body should be filled
With all graces wide-enlarged.
 Nature presently distilled
Helen's cheek, but not her heart,
 Cleopatra's majesty,
Atalanta's better part,
 Sad Lucretia's modesty.
Thus Rosalind of many parts
 By heavenly synod was devised,
Of many faces, eyes, and hearts,
 To have the touches dearest prized.
Heaven would that she these gifts should have,
And I to live and die her slave.'

ROSALIND O most gentle Jupiter, what tedious homily of love have you wearied your parishioners with, and never cried, 'Have patience, good people'!

CELIA How now? Back, friends, Shepherd, go off a little. Go with him, fellow.

TOUCHSTONE Come, shepherd, let us make an honorable retreat; though not with bag and baggage, yet with scrip and scrippage.   *[Exit with Corin.]*

CELIA Did you hear these verses?

ROSALIND O, yes, I heard them all, and more too; for some of them had in them more feet than the verses would bear.

CELIA That's no matter. The feet might bear the verses.

ROSALIND Ay, but the feet were lame, and could not bear themselves without the verse, and therefore stood lamely in the verse.

CELIA But did you hear without wondering how your name should be hanged and carved upon these trees?

ROSALIND I was seven of the nine days out of the wonder before you came; for look here what I found on a palm tree. I was never so berhymed since Pythagoras' time that I was an Irish rat, which I can hardly remember.

CELIA   Know you who has done this?

ROSALIND   Is it a man?

CELIA   And a chain that you once wore, about his neck. Change you color?

ROSALIND   I pray you, who?

CELIA   O Lord, Lord, it is a hard matter for friends to meet; but mountains may be moved by earthquakes, and so encounter.

ROSALIND   Nay, but who is it?

CELIA   Is it possible?

ROSALIND   Nay, I pray you now with most petitionary vehemence, tell me who it is.

CELIA   O wonderful, wonderful, and most wonderful wonderful, and yet again wonderful, and after that, out of all measure!

ROSALIND   Good my complexion! Do you think, though I am caparisoned like a man, I have a doublet and hose in my disposition? One inch of delay more is a South Sea of discovery. I pray, tell me who is it quickly, and speak apace. I would you could stammer, that you might pour this concealed man out of your mouth as wine comes out of a narrow-mouthed bottle; either too much at once, or none at all. I pray you, take the cork out of your mouth, that I may drink your tidings.

CELIA   So you may put a man in your belly.

ROSALIND   Is he of Good's making? What manner of man? Is his head worth a hat? or his chin worth a beard?

CELIA   Nay, he has but a little beard.

ROSALIND   Why, God will send more, if the man will be thankful. Let me stay the growth of his beard, if you delay me not the knowledge of his chin.

CELIA   It is young Orlando, that tripped up the wrestler's heels and your heart both in an instant.

ROSALIND   Nay, but the devil take mocking! Speak sad brow and true maid.

CELIA   In faith, cousin, it is he.

ROSALIND   Orlando?

CELIA   Orlando.

ROSALIND   Alas the day! what shall I do with my
    doublet and hose? What did he when you saw him? What
    said he? How looked he? Wherein went he? What makes
    he here? Did he ask for me? Where remains he? How
    parted he with you? and when shall you see him again?
    Answer me in one word.

CELIA   You must borrow me Gargantua's mouth first;
    it is a word too great for any mouth of this age's size. To
    say ay and no to these particulars is more than to answer
    in a catechism.

ROSALIND   But does he know that I am in this forest,
    and in man's apparel? Looks he as freshly as he did the
    day he wrestled?

CELIA   It is as easy to count motes as to resolve the
    propositions of a lover; but take a taste of my finding him,
    and relish it with good observance. I found him under a
    tree, like a dropped acorn.

ROSALIND   It may well be called Jove's tree when it
    drops such fruit.

CELIA   Give me audience, good madam.

ROSALIND   Proceed.

CELIA   There lay he stretched along like a wounded
    knight.

ROSALIND   Though it is pity to see such a sight, it
    well becomes the ground.

CELIA   Cry 'holla' to your tongue, I pray; it curvets
    unseasonably. He was furnished like a hunter.

ROSALIND   O, ominous! he comes to kill my heart.

CELIA   I would sing my song without a burden. You
    bring me out of tune.

ROSALIND   Do you not know I am a woman? When I
    think, I must speak. Sweet, say on.

Enter ORLANDO *and* JAQUES.

CELIA   You bring me out. Soft. Comes he not here?

ROSALIND   'Tis he! Slink by, and note him.

JAQUES   I thank you for your company; but, good faith,

I had as soon have been myself alone.

ORLANDO   And so had I; but yet for fashion sake I thank you too for your society.

JAQUES   God be with you; let's meet as little as we can.

ORLANDO   I do desire we may be better strangers.

JAQUES   I pray you, mar no more trees with writing love songs in their barks.

ORLANDO   I pray you mar no more of my verses by reading them badly.

JAQUES   Rosalind is your love's name?

ORLANDO   Yes, just.

JAQUES   I do not like her name.

ORLANDO   There was no thought of pleasing you when she was christened.

JAQUES   What stature is she of?

ORLANDO   Just as high as my heart.

JAQUES   You are full of pretty answers. Have you not been acquainted with goldsmiths' wives, and conned them out of rings?

ORLANDO   Not so; but I answer you right painted cloth, from whence you have studied your questions.

JAQUES   You have a nimble wit; I think it was made of Atalanta's heels. Will you sit down with me? and we two will rail against our mistress the world and all our misery.

ORLANDO   I will chide no breather in the world but myself, against whom I know most faults.

JAQUES   The worst fault you have is to be in love.

ORLANDO   It is a fault I will not change for your best virtue. I am weary of you.

JAQUES   By my word, I was seeking for a fool when I found you.

ORLANDO   He is drowned in the brook. Look but in and you shall see him.

JAQUES   There I shall see my own figure.

ORLANDO   Which I take to be either a fool or a cipher.

JAQUES   I'll tarry no longer with you. Farewell, good Signior Love.

ORLANDO   I am glad of your departure. Adieu, good
  Monsieur Melancholy.   *Exit Jaques.*

ROSALIND   I will speak to him like a saucy lackey,
  and under that habit play the knave with him. Do you
  hear, forester?

ORLANDO   Very well. What would you?

ROSALIND   I pray you, what is it o'clock?

ORLANDO   You should ask me, what time of day.
  There's no clock in the forest.

ROSALIND   Then there is no true lover in the forest,
  else sighing every minute and groaning every hour would
  detect the lazy foot of Time as well as a clock.

ORLANDO   And why not the swift foot of Time? Had
  not that been as proper?

ROSALIND   By no means, sir. Time travels in divers
  paces with divers persons. I'll tell you whom Time
  ambles with, whom Time trots with, whom Time
  gallops with, and whom he stands still with.

ORLANDO   Pray, whom does he trot with?

ROSALIND   Surely, he trots hard with a young maid
  between the contract of her marriage and the day it is
  solemnized. If the interim is but a week, Time's pace is
  so hard that it seems the length of seven years.

ORLANDO   Whom ambles Time with?

ROSALIND   With a priest that lacks Latin and a rich
  man that has not the gout; for the one sleeps easily
  because he cannot study, and the other lives merrily
  because he feels no pain: the one lacking the burden of
  lean and wasteful learning, the other knowing no burden
  of heavy tedious penury. These Time ambles with.

ORLANDO   Whom does he gallop with?

ROSALIND   With a thief to the gallows; for though he
  goes as softly as foot can fall, he thinks himself too soon
  there.

ORLANDO   Whom stays it still with?

ROSALIND   With lawyers in the vacation; for they
  sleep between term and term, and then they perceive not
  how time moves.

ORLANDO   Where dwell you, pretty youth?

ROSALIND   With this shepherdess, my sister; here in the skirts of the forest, like fringe upon a petticoat.

ORLANDO   Are you native of this place?

ROSALIND   As the rabbit that you see dwell where she is kindled.

ORLANDO   Your accent is something finer than you could purchase in so removed a dwelling.

ROSALIND   I have been told so of many. But indeed an old religious uncle of mine taught me to speak, who was in his youth a well bred man; one that knew courtship too well, for he fell in love. I have heard him read many lectures against it; and I thank God I am not a woman, to be touched with so many giddy offenses as he has generally taxed their whole sex with.

ORLANDO   Can you remember any of the principal evils that he laid to the charge of women?

ROSALIND   There were none principal. They were all like one another as halfpence are, every one fault seeming monstrous till his fellow-fault came to match it.

ORLANDO   I pray you, recount some of them.

ROSALIND   No, I will not cast away my physic but on those that are sick. There is a man haunts the forest that abuses our young plants with carving 'Rosalind' on their barks, hangs odes upon hawthorns, and elegies on brambles; all, forsooth, deifying the name of Rosalind. If I could meet that fancy-monger, I would give him some good counsel, for he seems to have the fever of love upon him.

ORLANDO   I am he that is so love-shaked. I pray you tell me your remedy.

ROSALIND   There is none of my uncle's marks upon you. He taught me how to know a man in love; in which cage of rushes I am sure you are not a prisoner.

ORLANDO   What were his marks?

ROSALIND   A lean cheek, which you have not; a blue eye and sunken, which you have not; an unconversible spirit, which you have not; a beard neglected, which you

have not. But I pardon you for that, for simply your
having small beard is a brother's revenue. Then your hose
should be ungartered, your bonnet unbanded, your sleeve
unbuttoned, your shoe untied, and everything about you
demonstrating a careless desolation. But you are no such
man: you are rather precise in your accoutrements, as
loving yourself than seeming the lover of any other.

ORLANDO   Fair youth, I would I could make you
believe I love.

ROSALIND   Me believe it? You may as soon make her
that you love believe it, which I warrant she is apter to do
than to confess she does. That is one of the points in
which women ever give the lie to their consciences. But
in good truth, are you he that hangs the verses on the
trees wherein Rosalind is so admired?

ORLANDO   I swear to you, youth, by the white hand
of Rosalind, I am that he, that unfortunate he.

ROSALIND   But are you so much in love as your
rhymes speak?

ORLANDO   Neither rhyme nor reason can express how
much.

ROSALIND   Love is merely a madness, and, I tell you,
deserves as well a dark house and a whip as madmen do.
And the reason why they are not so punished and cured
is that the lunacy is so ordinary that the whippers are in
love too. Yet I profess curing it by counsel.

ORLANDO   Did you ever cure any so?

ROSALIND   Yes, one, and in this manner. He was to
imagine me his love, his mistress; and I set him every day
to woo me. At which time would I, being but a moonish
youth, grieve, be effeminate, changeable, longing and
liking, proud, fantastical, apish, shallow, inconstant, full
of tears, full of smiles. For every passion something and
for no passion truly anything, as boys and women are for
the most part cattle of this color; would now like him,
now loathe him; then entertain him, then forswear him;
now weep for him, then spit at him. That I drove my
suitor from his mad humor of love to a living humor of

madness: which was, to forswear the full stream of the
world and to live in a nook merely monastic. And thus I
cured him; and this way will I take upon me to wash your
liver as clean as a sound sheep's heart, that there shall not
be one spot of love in it.

ORLANDO   I would not be cured, youth.

ROSALIND   I would cure you, if you would but call
me Rosalind and come every day to my cottage and woo
me.

ORLANDO   Now, by the faith of my love, I will. Tell
me where it is.

ROSALIND   Go with me to it, and I'll show it you;
and by the way you shall tell me where in the forest you
live. Will you go?

ORLANDO   With all my heart, good youth.

ROSALIND   Nay, you must call me Rosalind. Come,
sister, will you go?   *Exeunt.*

SCENE III
Another part of the Forest.

Enter TOUCHSTONE *the Clown,* AUDREY; *and*
JAQUES *following.*

TOUCHSTONE   Come apace, good Audrey. I will fetch up
your goats, Audrey. And how, Audrey, am I the man yet?
Do my simple features content you?

AUDREY   Your features, Lord warrant us! What features?

TOUCHSTONE   I am here with you and your goats as the
most goatish poet, honest Ovid, was among the Goths.

JAQUES   [*aside*] O knowledge ill-inhabited, worse than
Jove in a thatched house!

TOUCHSTONE   When a man's verses cannot be understood,
nor a man's good wit seconded with the forward child,
understanding, it strikes a man more dead than a great
reckoning in a little room. Truly, I would the gods had
made you poetical.

AUDREY   I do not know what poetical is. Is it honest in deed and word? Is it a true thing?

TOUCHSTONE   No, truly; for the truest poetry is the most faining, and lovers are given to poetry, and what they swear in poetry may be said, as lovers, they do feign.

AUDREY   Do you wish then that the gods had made me poetical?

TOUCHSTONE   I do truly; for you swear to me you are honest. Now if you were a poet, I might have some hope you did feign.

AUDREY   Would you not have me honest?

TOUCHSTONE   No, truly, unless you were ill-looking: for honesty coupled to beauty is to have honey a sauce to sugar.

JAQUES   [aside] A sensible fool.

AUDREY   Well, I am not fair, and therefore I pray the gods make me honest.

TOUCHSTONE   Truly, and to cast away honesty upon a foul slut were to put good meat into an unclean dish.

AUDREY   I am not a slut, though I thank the gods I am foul.

TOUCHSTONE   Well, praised be the gods for your foulness! Sluttishness may come hereafter. But be it as it may be, I will marry you; and to that end I have been with Sir Oliver Martext, the vicar of the next village, who has promised to meet me in this place of the forest and to couple us.

JAQUES   [aside] I would fain see this meeting.

AUDREY   Well, the gods give us joy!

TOUCHSTONE   Amen. A man may, if he were of a fearful heart, stagger in this attempt; for here we have no temple but the wood, no assembly but horn-beasts. But what though? Courage! As horns are odious, they are necessary. It is said, 'Many a man knows no end of his goods.' Right! Many a man has good horns and knows no end of them. Well, that is the dowry of his wife; 'tis none of his own getting. Horns? Even so, poor men alone? No, no; the noblest deer has them as huge as the poorest. Is the single man therefore blessed? No; as a walled town is more worthy than a village, so is the forehead of a married man more honorable than the bare brow of a bachelor. And by how much defense is better than no skill, by so much is a horn more precious than to want one.

Enter SIR OLIVER MARTEXT.

Here comes Sir Oliver. Sir Oliver Martext, you are well met. Will you dispatch us here under this tree, or shall we go with you to your chapel?

MARTEXT   Is there none here to give the woman?

TOUCHSTONE   I will not take her on gift of any man.

MARTEXT   Truly, she must be given, or the marriage is not lawful.

JAQUES   [*comes forward*] Proceed, proceed; I'll give her.

TOUCHSTONE   Good even, good Master What-ye-call it. How do you, sir? You are very well met. God yield you for your last company; I am very glad to see you. Even a toy in hand here, sir. Nay, pray be hatted.

JAQUES   Will you be married, motley?

TOUCHSTONE   As the ox has his yoke, sir, the horse his curb, and the falcon her bells, so man has his desires; and as pigeons bill, so wedlock would be nibbling.

JAQUES   And will you, being a man of your breeding, be married under a bush like a beggar? Get you to church, and have a good priest that can tell you what marriage is. This fellow will but join you together as they join wainscot; then one of you will prove a shrunk panel, and like green timber, warp, warp.

TOUCHSTONE   [*aside*] I am not in the mind; but I were better to be married by him than by another; for he is not likely to marry me well. And not being well married, it will be a good excuse for me hereafter to leave my wife.

JAQUES   Go you with me and let me counsel you.

TOUCHSTONE   Come, sweet Audrey. We must be married,
or we must live in bawdry, Farewell, good Master Oliver:
not

> O sweet Oliver,
> O brave Oliver,
> Leave me not behind you;

but

> Wind away,
> Be gone, I say;
> I will not to wedding with you.

Exeunt Jaques, Touchstone, and Audrey.

MARTEXT   It is no matter. Never a fantastical knave of
them all shall flout me out of my calling.   *[Exit.]*

SCENE IV
Another part of the Forest.

Enter ROSALIND *and* CELIA.

ROSALIND   Never talk to me; I will weep.

CELIA   Do, I pray; but yet have the grace to consider that
tears do not become a man.

ROSALIND   But have I not cause to weep?

CELIA   As good cause as one would desire; therefore weep.

ROSALIND   His very hair is of the dissembling color.

CELIA   Something browner than Judas's. Indeed, his
kisses are Judas's own children.

ROSALIND   In faith, his hair is of a good color.

CELIA   An excellent color. Your chestnut was ever the
only color.

ROSALIND   And his kissing is as full of sanctity as the
touch of holy bread.

CELIA   He has bought a pair of cast lips of Diana. A nun
of winter's sisterhood kisses not more religiously; the
very ice of chastity is in them.

ROSALIND   But why did he swear he would come this
morning, and comes not?

CELIA Nay, certainly there is no truth in him.

ROSALIND Do you think so?

CELIA Yes; I think he is not a pickpurse nor a horse-stealer, but for his verity in love, I do think him as concave as a covered goblet or a worm-eaten nut.

ROSALIND Not true in love?

CELIA Yes, when he is in, but I think he is not in.

ROSALIND You have heard him swear downright he was.

CELIA 'Was' is not 'is'. Besides, the oath of a lover is no stronger than the word of a tapster; they are both the confirmer of false reckonings. He attends here in the forest on the Duke your father.

ROSALIND I met the Duke yesterday and had much question with him. He asked me of what parentage I was. I told him, of as good as he; so he laughed and let me go. But what talk we of fathers when there is such a man as Orlando?

CELIA O, that's a brave man; he writes brave verses, speaks brave words, swears brave oaths, and breaks them bravely. Quite traverse, athwart the heart of his lover, as a puny tilter, that spurs his horse but on one side, breaks his staff like a noble goose. But all is brave that youth mounts and folly guides. Who comes here?

Enter CORIN.

CORIN
Mistress and Master, you have oft enquired
After the shepherd that complained of love,
Whom you saw sitting by me on the turf,
Praising the proud disdainful shepherdess
That was his mistress.

CELIA   Well, and what of him?

CORIN
If you will see a pageant truly played
Between the pale complexion of true love
And the red glow of scorn and proud disdain,

Go hence a little, and I shall conduct you,
If you will mark it.

ROSALIND O, come, let us remove:
The sight of lovers feeds well those in love.
Bring us to this sight, and you shall say
I'll prove a busy actor in their play. *Exeunt.*

SCENE V
Another part of the Forest.

Enter SILVIUS *and* PHEBE.

SILVIUS
Sweet Phebe, do not scorn me; do not, Phebe!
Say that you love me not, but say not so
In bitterness. The common executioner,
Whose heart the accustomed sight of death makes
hard,
Drops not the axe upon the humbled neck
But first begs pardon. Will you sterner be
Than he that dies and lives by bloody drops?

Enter ROSALIND, CELIA, *and* CORIN *behind.*

PHEBE
I would not be your executioner.
I fly you, for I would not injure you.
You tell me there is murder in my eye:
'Tis pretty, sure, and very probable
That eyes, that are the frailest and softest things,
Which shut their coward gates on tiny motes,
Should be called tyrants, butchers, murderers.
Now I do frown on you with all my heart,
And if my eyes can wound, now let them kill you.
Now counterfeit to swoon; why, now fall down;
Or if you can not, O, for shame, for shame,
Lie not, to say my eyes are murderers.

Now show the wound my eye has made in you;
Scratch yourself with a pin, and there remains
Some scar of it; lean upon a rush,
The trace and visible impression of it
Your palm some moment keeps. But now my eyes,
Which I have darted at you, hurt you not,
And I am sure there is no force in eyes
That can do hurt.

SILVIUS   O dear Phebe,
If ever, as that ever may be near,
You meet in some fresh cheek the power of fancy,
Then shall you know the wounds invisible
That love's keen arrows make.

PHEBE   But till that time
Come you not near me; and when that time comes,
Afflict me with your mocks, pity me not,
As till that time I shall not pity you.

ROSALIND
And why, I pray you? Who might be your mother,
That you insult, exult, and all at once,
Over the wretched? What though you have no beauty—
As, by my faith, I see no more in you
Than without candle may go dark to bed—
Must you be therefore proud and pitiless?
Why, what means this? Why do you look on me?
I see no more in you than in the ordinary
Of nature's ready-made. 'Od's my little life,
I think she means to tangle my eyes too!
No, faith, proud mistress, hope not after it;
'Tis not your inky brows, your black silk hair,
Your bugle eyeballs, nor your cheek of cream
That can entame my spirits to your worship.
You foolish shepherd, wherefore do you follow her,
Like foggy south, puffing with wind and rain?
You are a thousand times a handsomer man
Than she a woman. 'Tis such fools as you
That make the world full of ill-looking children.
'Tis not her glass, but you, that flatters her.

And out of you she sees herself more decent
Than any of her lineaments can show her.
But mistress, know yourself. Down on your knees,
And thank heaven, fasting, for a good man's love.
For I must tell you friendly in your ear,
Sell when you can, you are not for all markets.
Cry the man mercy, love him, take his offer;
Foul is most foul, being foul to be a scoffer;
So take her to you, shepherd. Fare you well.

PHEBE
Sweet youth, I pray you chide a year together;
I had rather hear you chide than this man woo.

ROSALIND   [aside] He's fallen in love with your foulness,
and she'll fall in love with my anger. If it is so, as fast as
she answers you with frowning looks, I'll sauce her with
bitter words. [to Phebe] Why look you so upon me?

PHEBE
For no ill will I bear you.

ROSALIND
I pray you do not fall in love with me,
For I am falser than vows made in wine.
Besides, I like you not. If you will know my house,
'Tis at the tuft of olives, here hard by.
Will you go, sister? Shepherd, ply her hard.
Come, sister. Shepherdess, look on him better
And be not proud. Though all the world could see,
None could be so abused in sight as he.
Come, to our flock.   Exit with Celia and Corin.

PHEBE
Dead shepherd, now I find your phrase of might,
'Who ever loved that loved not at first sight?'

SILVIUS
Sweet Phebe.

PHEBE   Ha! what say you, Silvius?

SILVIUS
Sweet Phebe, pity me.

PHEBE
Why, I am sorry for you, gentle Silvius.

SILVIUS

    Wherever sorrow is, relief would be.
    If you do sorrow at my grief in love,
    By giving love your sorrow and my grief
    Were both exterminated.

PHEBE

    You have my love. Is not that neighborly?

SILVIUS

    I would have you.

PHEBE   Why, that were covetousness
    Silvius, the time was that I hated you;
    And yet it is not that I bear you love,
    But since now you can talk of love so well,
    Your company, which once was irksome to me,
    I will endure; and I'll employ you too.
    But do not look for further recompense
    Than your own gladness that you are employed.

SILVIUS

    So holy and so perfect is my love,
    And I in such a poverty of grace,
    That I shall think it a most plenteous crop
    To glean the broken ears after the man
    That the main harvest reaps. Loose now and then
    A scattered smile, and that I'll live upon.

PHEBE

    Know you the youth that spoke to me erewhile?

SILVIUS

    Not very well, but I have met him oft,
    And he has bought the cottage and the bounds
    That the old peasant once was master of.

PHEBE

    Think not I love him, though I ask for him;
    'Tis but a peevish boy; yet he talks well.
    But what care I for words? Yet words do well
    When he that speaks them pleases those that hear.
    It is a pretty youth; not very pretty;
    But sure he's proud; and yet his pride becomes him.
    He'll make a proper man. The best thing in him

Is his complexion; and faster than his tongue
Did make offense, his eye did heal it up.
He is not very tall; yet for his years he's tall.
His leg is but so so; and yet 'tis well.
There was a pretty redness in his lip,
A little riper and more lusty red
Than that mixed in his cheek. 'Twas just the difference
Between the constant red and mingled damask.
There are some women, Silvius, had they marked him
In parcels as I did, would have gone near
To fall in love with him. But, for my part,
I love him not and hate him not; and yet
I have more cause to hate him than to love him;
For what had he to do to chide at me?
He said my eyes were black and my hair black;
And, now I have remembered, scorned at me.
I marvel why I answered not again.
But that's all one: omittance is no quittance.
I'll write to him a very taunting letter,
And you shall bear it. Will you, Silvius?

SILVIUS
Phebe, with all my heart.

PHEBE   I'll write it straight;
The matter's in my head and in my heart;
I will be bitter with him and passing short.
Go with me, Silvius.   *Exeunt.*

Act IV

❀

SCENE I
The Forest of Arden.

Enter ROSALIND, CELIA *and* JAQUES.

JAQUES I pray, pretty youth, let me be better acquainted with you.

ROSALIND They say you are a melancholy fellow.

JAQUES I am so; I do love it better than laughing.

ROSALIND Those that are in extremity of either are abominable fellows, and betray themselves to every modern censure worse than drunkards.

JAQUES Why, it is good to be sad and say nothing.

ROSALIND Why then, it is good to be a post.

JAQUES I have neither the scholar's melancholy, which is emulation; nor the musician's, which is fantastical; nor the courtier's, which is proud; nor the soldier's, which is ambitious; nor the lawyer's, which is politic; nor the lady's, which is refined; nor the lover's, which is all these. But it is a melancholy of my own, compounded of many simples, extracted from many objects; and indeed the sundry contemplation of my travels, which, by often rumination, wraps me in a most moody sadness.

ROSALIND A traveller! By my faith, you have great reason to be sad. I fear you have sold your own lands to see other men's. Then to have seen much and to have nothing is to have rich eyes and poor hands.

JAQUES Yes, I have gained my experience.

Enter ORLANDO.

ROSALIND   And your experience makes you sad. I had
  rather have a fool to make me merry than experience to
  make me sad: and to travel for it too.

ORLANDO   Good day and happiness, dear Rosalind.

JAQUES   Nay then, God be with you, if you talk in blank
  verse.

ROSALIND   Farewell, Monsieur Traveller. Look you lisp
  and wear strange suits, disparage all the benefits of your
  own country; be out of love with your nativity, and
  almost chide God for making you that countenance you
  are, or I will scarce think you have swum in a gondola.
                                              [Exit Jaques.]
  Why, how now, Orlando, where have you been all this
  while? You a lover? If you serve me such another trick,
  never come in my sight more.

ORLANDO   My fair Rosalind, I come within an hour of
  my promise.

ROSALIND   Break an hour's promise in love? He that will
  divide a minute into a thousand parts and break but a
  part of the thousandth part of a minute in the affairs of
  love, it may be said of him that Cupid has clapped him on
  the shoulder, but I'll warrant him heart-whole.

ORLANDO   Pardon me, dear Rosalind.

ROSALIND   Nay, if you are so tardy, come no more in my
  sight. I had as soon be wooed by a snail.

ORLANDO   By a snail?

ROSALIND   Ay, by a snail; for though he comes slowly, he
  carries his house on his head; a better jointure, I think,
  than you make a woman. Besides, he brings his destiny
  with him.

ORLANDO   What's that?

ROSALIND   Why, horns; which such as you are fain to be
  beholding to your wives for; but he comes armed in his
  fortune and forestalls the slander of his wife.

ORLANDO   Virtue is no horn-maker, and my Rosalind is
  virtuous.

ROSALIND   And I am your Rosalind.

CELIA   It pleases him to call you so; but he has a Rosalind
of a better leer than you.

ROSALIND   Come, woo me, woo me; for now I am in a
holiday humor and like enough to consent. What would
you say to me now, if I were your very very Rosalind?

ORLANDO   I would kiss before I spoke.

ROSALIND   Nay, you were better speak first, and when
you were gravelled for lack of matter, you might take
occasion to kiss. Very good orators, when they are out,
they will spit; and for lovers, lacking—God warn us!—
matter, the cleanliest shift is to kiss.

ORLANDO   How if the kiss is denied?

ROSALIND   Then she puts you to entreaty, and there
begins new matter.

ORLANDO   Who could be out, being before his beloved
mistress?

ROSALIND   Indeed, that should you, if I were your
mistress, or I should think my honesty ranker than my
wit.

ORLANDO   What, of my suit?

ROSALIND   Not out of your apparel, and yet out of your
suit. Am not I your Rosalind?

ORLANDO   I take some joy to say you are, because I
would be talking of her.

ROSALIND   Well, in her person, I say I will not have you.

ORLANDO   Then, in my own person, I die.

ROSALIND   No, faith, die by attorney. The poor world is
almost six thousand years old, and in all this time there
was not any man died in his own person, that is to say, in
a love cause. Troilus had his brains dashed out by a
Grecian club; yet he did what he could to die before, and
he is one of the patterns of love. Leander, he would have
lived many a fair year though Hero had turned nun, if it
had not been for a hot midsummer night. For, good
youth, he went but forth to wash him in the Hellespont,
and being taken with the cramp, was drowned; and the
foolish chroniclers of that age found it was 'Hero of

Sestos.' But these are all lies. Men have died from time to time, and worms have eaten them, but not for love.

ORLANDO   I would not have my right Rosalind of this mind, for I protest her frown might kill me.

ROSALIND   By this hand, it will not kill a fly. But come, now I will be your Rosalind in a more coming-on disposition; and ask me what you will, I will grant it.

ORLANDO   Then love me, Rosalind.

ROSALIND   Yes, faith, will I, Fridays and Saturdays and all.

ORLANDO   And will you have me?

ROSALIND   Ay, and twenty such.

ORLANDO   What say you?

ROSALIND   Are you not good?

ORLANDO   I hope so.

ROSALIND   Why then, can one desire too much of a good thing? Come, sister, you shall be the priest and marry us. Give me your hand, Orlando. What do you say, sister?

ORLANDO   Pray you marry us.

CELIA   I cannot say the words.

ROSALIND   You must begin, 'Will you, Orlando'—

CELIA   Go to. Will you, Orlando, have to wife this Rosalind?

ORLANDO   I will.

ROSALIND   Ay, but when?

ORLANDO   Why now, as fast as she can marry us.

ROSALIND   Then you must say, 'I take you, Rosalind, for wife.'

ORLANDO   I take you, Rosalind, for wife.

ROSALIND   I might ask you for your commission; but I do take you, Orlando, for my husband. There's a girl goes before the priest, and certainly a woman's thought runs before her actions.

ORLANDO   So do all thoughts; they are winged.

ROSALIND   Now tell me how long you would have her after you have possessed her.

ORLANDO   For ever and a day.

ROSALIND   Say 'a day,' without the 'ever.' No, no,

Orlando; men are April when they woo, December when they wed. Maids are May when they are maids, but the sky changes when they are wives. I will be more jealous of you than a Barbary cock-pigeon over his hen, more clamorous than a parrot against rain, more newfangled than an ape, more giddy in my desires than a monkey. I will weep for nothing, like Diana in the fountain, and I will do that when you are disposed to be merry; I will laugh like a hyena, and that when you are inclined to sleep.

ORLANDO   But will my Rosalind do so?

ROSALIND   By my life, she will do as I do.

ORLANDO   O, but she is wise.

ROSALIND   Or else she could not have the wit to do this; the wiser, the waywarder. Make the doors upon a woman's wit, and it will out at the casement; shut that, and it will out at the keyhole; stop that, it will fly with the smoke out at the chimney.

ORLANDO   A man that had a wife with such a wit, he might say, 'Wit, whither will it?'

ROSALIND   Nay, you might keep that check for it till you met your wife's wit going to your neighbor's bed.

ORLANDO   And what wit could wit have to excuse that?

ROSALIND   Surely, to say she came to seek you there. You shall never take her without her answer, unless you take her without her tongue. O, that woman that cannot make her fault her husband's occasion, let her never nurse her child herself, for she will breed it like a fool.

ORLANDO   For these two hours, Rosalind, I will leave you.

ROSALIND   Alas, dear love, I cannot lack you two hours!

ORLANDO   I must attend the Duke at dinner. By two o'clock I will be with you again.

ROSALIND   Ay, go your ways, go your ways; I knew what you would prove. My friends told me as much, and I thought no less. That flattering tongue of yours won me. It is but one cast away, and so, come death! Two o'clock is your hour?

ORLANDO   Ay, sweet Rosalind.

ROSALIND   By my word, and in good earnest, and so God
mend me, and by all pretty oaths that are not dangerous,
if you break one jot of your promise or come one minute
behind your hour, I will think you the most pathetical
break-promise, and the most hollow lover, and the most
unworthy of her you call Rosalind, that may be chosen
out of the gross band of the unfaithful. Therefore beware
my censure and keep your promise.

ORLANDO   With no less religion than if you were indeed
my Rosalind. So adieu.

ROSALIND   Well, Time is the old justice that examines
all such offenders, and let Time try. Adieu.

Exit Orlando.

CELIA   You have simply misused our sex in your love-
prate. We must have your doublet and hose plucked over
your head, and show the world what the bird has done to
her own nest.

ROSALIND   O cousin, my pretty little cousin, that you
did know how many fathom deep I am in love! But it
cannot be sounded. My affection has an unknown
bottom, like the Bay of Portugal.

CELIA   Or rather, bottomless, that as fast as you pour
affection in, it runs out.

ROSALIND   No, that same wicked bastard of Venus that
was begot of thought, conceived of spleen, and born of
madness, that blind rascally boy that abuses every one's
eyes because his own are out, let him be judge how deep
I am in love. I tell you, Aliena, I cannot be out of the sight
of Orlando. I'll go find a shadow, and sigh till he comes.

CELIA   And I'll sleep.   *Exeunt.*

SCENE II
Another part of the Forest.

Enter JAQUES, LORDS *and* FORESTERS.

JAQUES   Which is he that killed the deer?

A LORD   Sir, it was I.

JAQUES   Let's present him to the Duke like a Roman
conqueror; and it would do well to set the deer's horns
upon his head for a branch of victory. Have you no song,
forester, for this purpose?

FORESTER   Yes, sir.

JAQUES   Sing it. It is no matter how it is in tune, if it
makes noise enough.

    Music.

Song.

What shall he have that killed the deer?
His leather skin and horns to wear:
    Then sing him home. *[The rest shall bear this burden.]*
Take you no scorn to wear the horn,
It was a crest ere you were born,
    Your father's father wore it,
    And your father bore it.
The horn, the horn, the lusty horn,
Is not a thing to laugh to scorn.   *Exeunt.*

SCENE III
Another part of the Forest.

Enter ROSALIND *and* CELIA.

ROSALIND   How say you now, is it not past two o'clock?
And here much Orlando!

CELIA   I warrent you, with pure love and troubled brain,
he has taken his bow and arrows and gone forth to sleep.

Enter SILVIUS.

Look who comes here.

SILVIUS

My errand is to you, fair youth.
My gentle Phebe did bid me give you this.

[Gives a letter.]

I know not the contents, but, as I guess
By the stern brow and waspish action
Which she did use as she was writing of it,
It bears an angry tenor. Pardon me;
I am but as a guiltless messenger.

ROSALIND

Patience herself would startle at this letter
And play the swaggerer. Bear this, bear all!
She says I am not fair, that I lack manners;
She calls me proud, and that she could not love me,
Were man as rare as phoenix. 'Od's my will!
Her love is not the hare that I do hunt.
Why writes she so to me? Well, shepherd, well,
This is a letter of your own device.

SILVIUS

No, I protest, I know not the contents.
Phebe did write it.

ROSALIND   Come, come, you are a fool,
And turned into the extremity of love.
I saw her hand. She has a leathern hand,
A freestone-colored hand. I verily did think
That her old gloves were on, but 'twas her hands.
She has a housewife's hand; but that's no matter:
I say she never did invent this letter;
This is a man's invention and his hand.

SILVIUS

Sure it is hers.

ROSALIND

Why, 'tis a boisterous and a cruel style,
A style for challengers. Why, she defies me
Like Turk to Christian. Women's gentle brain
Could not drop forth such giant-rude invention,
Such Ethiop words, blacker in their effect
Than in their countenance. Will you hear the letter?

SILVIUS

So please you, for I never heard it yet;
Yet heard too much of Phebe's cruelty.

ROSALIND

She Phebes me. Mark how the tyrant writes.
(Read.) 'Are you god, to shepherd turned,
          That a maiden's heart has burned?'
Can a woman rail thus?

SILVIUS   Call you this railing?

ROSALIND

(Read.) 'Why, your godhead laid apart,
          War you with a woman's heart?'
Did you ever hear such railing?
          'While the eye of man did woo me,
          That could do no vengeance to me.'
‾Meaning me a beast.
          'If the scorn of your bright eyne [eyes]
          Has power to raise such love in mine,
          Alas, in me what strange effect
          Would they work in mild aspect!
          While you chid me, I did love;
          How then might your prayèrs move!
          He that brings this love to thee
          Little knows this love in me;
          And by him seal up your mind,
          Whether that your youth and kind
          Will the faithful offer take
          Of me and all that I can make,
          Or else by him my love deny,
          And then I'll study how to die.'

SILVIUS

Call you this chiding?

CELIA   Alas, poor shepherd!

ROSALIND Do you pity him? No, he deserves no pity.
Will you love such a woman? What, to make you an
instrument, and play false strains upon you? Not to be

endured! Well, go your way to her, for I see love has made
you a tame snake, and say this to her: that if she loves me,
I charge her to love you; if she will not, I will never have
her unless you entreat for her. If you are a true lover,
hence, and not a word; for here comes more company.
Exit Silvius.

Enter OLIVER.

OLIVER

Good morrow, fair ones. Pray you, if you know,
Where in the purlieus of this forest stands
A sheepcote, fenced about with olive trees?

CELIA

West of this place, down in the neighbor bottom.
The rank of osiers by the murmuring stream
Left on your right hand brings you to the place.
But at this hour the house does keep itself;
There's none within.

OLIVER

If now an eye may profit by a tongue,
Then should I know you by description,
Such garments and such years: 'The boy is fair,
Of female feature, and bestows himself
Like a ripe sister; the woman low,
And browner than her brother.' Are not you
The owner of the house I did enquire for?

CELIA

It is no boast, being asked, to say we are.

OLIVER

Orlando does commend him to you both,
And to that youth he calls his Rosalind
He sends this bloody napkin. Are you he?

ROSALIND

I am. What must we understand by this?

OLIVER

Some of my shame, if you will know of me
What man I am, and how and why and where

This handkerchief was stained.

CELIA   I pray you tell it.

OLIVER

When last the young Orlando parted from you,
He left a promise to return again
Within an hour; and pacing through the forest,
Chewing the food of sweet and bitter fancy,
Lo, what befell! He threw his eye aside,
And mark what object did present itself:
Under an old oak, whose boughs were mossed with age
And high top bald with dry antiquity,
A wretched ragged man, o'ergrown with hair,
Lay sleeping on his back. About his neck
A green and gilded snake had wreathed itself,
Which with its head, nimble in threats, approached
The opening of his mouth. But suddenly,
Seeing Orlando, it unlinked itself
And with indented glides did slip away
Into a bush. Under which bush's shade
A lioness, with udders all drawn dry,
Lay couching, head on ground, with catlike watch
For when the sleeping man should stir. For 'tis
The royal disposition of that beast
To prey on nothing that does seem as dead.
This seen, Orlando did approach the man
And found it was his brother, his elder brother.

CELIA

O, I have heard him speak of that same brother,
And he did render him the most unnatural
That lived among men.

OLIVER   And well he might so do,
For well I know he was unnatural.

ROSALIND

But, to Orlando: did he leave him there,
Food to the sucked and hungry lioness?

OLIVER

Twice did he turn his back and purposed so;
But kindness, nobler ever than revenge,

And nature, stronger than his just occasion,
Made him give battle to the lioness,
Which quickly fell before him. In which horror
From miserable slumber I awaked.

CELIA
Are you his brother?

ROSALIND   Was it you he rescued?

CELIA
Was it you that did so oft contrive to kill him?

OLIVER
It was I. But 'tis not I. I do not shame
To tell you what I was, since my conversion
So sweetly tastes, being the thing I am.

ROSALIND
But, for the bloody napkin?

OLIVER   By and by.
When from the first to last, between us two,
Tears our recital had most kindly bathed,
As how I came into that desert place.
In brief, he led me to the gentle Duke,
Who gave me fresh array and entertainment,
Committing me unto my brother's love:
Who led me instantly unto his cave,
There stripped himself, and here upon his arm
The lioness had torn some flesh away,
Which all this while had bled. And now he fainted,
And cried, in fainting, upon Rosalind.
Brief, I recovered him, bound up his wound.
And after some small space, being strong at heart,
He sent me hither, stranger as I am,
To tell this story, that you might excuse
His broken promise, and to give this napkin,
Dyed in his blood, unto the shepherd youth
That he in sport does call his Rosalind.

[Rosalind faints.]

CELIA

Why, how now, Ganymede, sweet Ganymede!

OLIVER

Many will swoon when they do look on blood.

CELIA

There is more in it. Cousin Ganymede!

OLIVER

Look, he recovers.

ROSALIND

I would I were at home.

CELIA   We'll lead you thither.

I pray you, will you take him by the arm?

OLIVER   Be of good cheer, youth. You a man! You lack a
man's heart.

ROSALIND   I do so, I confess it. Ah, man, a body would
think this was well counterfeited. I pray you tell your
brother how well I counterfeited. Heigh-ho!

OLIVER   This was not counterfeit. There is too great
testimony in your complexion that it was a passion of
earnest.

ROSALIND   Counterfeit, I assure you.

OLIVER   Well then, take a good heart and counterfeit to
be a man.

ROSALIND   So I do; but in faith, I should have been a
woman by right.

CELIA   Come, you look paler and paler. Pray you draw
homewards. Good sir, go with us.

OLIVER

That will I, for I must bear answer back

How you excuse my brother, Rosalind.

ROSALIND   I shall devise something. But I pray you
commend my counterfeiting to him. Will you go?

                              Exeunt.

Act V

❀

SCENE I
The Forest of Arden.

Enter TOUCHSTONE *and* AUDREY.

TOUCHSTONE   We shall find a time, Audrey. Patience gentle Audrey.

AUDREY   Faith, the priest was good enough, for all the old gentleman's saying.

TOUCHSTONE   A most wicked Sir Oliver, Audrey, a most vile Martext. But, Audrey, there is a youth here in the forest lays claim to you.

AUDREY   Ay, I know who it is. He has no interest in me in the world. Here comes the man you mean.

Enter WILLIAM.

TOUCHSTONE   It is meat and drink to me to see a clown; by my word, we that have good wits have much to answer for. We shall be flouting; we cannot hold tongue.

WILLIAM   Good even, Audrey.

AUDREY   God give you good even, William.

WILLIAM   And good even to you, sir.

TOUCHSTONE   Good even, gentle friend. Cover your head, cover your head. Nay, pray be covered. How old are you, friend?

WILLIAM   Five-and-twenty, sir.

TOUCHSTONE   A ripe age. Is your name William?

WILLIAM   William, sir.

TOUCHSTONE   A fair name. Born in the forest here?

WILLIAM   Ay, sir, I thank God.

TOUCHSTONE   'Thank God.' A good answer. Are you rich?

WILLIAM   Fair, sir, so so.

TOUCHSTONE   'So so' is good, very good, very excellent good; and yet it is not, it is but so so. Are you wise?

WILLIAM   Ay, sir, I have a pretty wit.

TOUCHSTONE   Why, you say well. I do now remember a saying, 'The fool does think he is wise, but the wise man knows himself to be a fool.' The heathen philosopher, when he had a desire to eat a grape, would open his lips when he put it into his mouth, meaning thereby that grapes were made to eat and lips to open. You do love this maid?

WILLIAM   I do, sir.

TOUCHSTONE   Give me your hand. Are you learned?

WILLIAM   No, sir.

TOUCHSTONE   Then learn this of me: to have is to have; for it is a figure in rhetoric that drink, being poured out of a cup into a glass, by filling the one does empty the other; for all your writers do consent that *ipse* [himself] is he. Now, you are not *ipse*, for I am he.

WILLIAM   Which he, sir?

TOUCHSTONE   He, sir, that must marry this woman. Therefore, you clown, abandon (which is in the vulgar, leave) the society (which in the boorish is, company) of this female (which in the common is, woman). Which together is, abandon the society of this female, or, clown, you perish; or, to your better understanding, die. Or, to wit, I kill you, make you away, translate your life into death, your liberty into bondage. I will deal in poison with you, or in bastinado, or in steel; I will bandy with you in faction; I will overrun you with policy; I will kill you a hundred and fifty ways. Therefore tremble and depart.

AUDREY   Do, good William.

WILLIAM   God rest you, merry sir.   *Exit.*

Enter CORIN.

CORIN   Our master and mistress seek you. Come away,
   away!
TOUCHSTONE   Trip, Audrey, trip, Audrey. I attend, I attend.
                                                          Exeunt.

SCENE II
Another part of the Forest.

Enter ORLANDO *and* OLIVER.

ORLANDO   Is it possible that on so little acquaintance
   you should like her? that but seeing, you should love her?
   and loving, woo? and wooing, she should grant? And will
   you persevere to enjoy her?
OLIVER   Neither call the giddiness of it in question, the
   poverty of her, the small acquaintance, my sudden
   wooing, nor her sudden consenting. But say with me, I
   love Aliena; say with her that she loves me; consent with
   both that we may enjoy each other. It shall be to your
   good; for my father's house, and all the revenue that was
   old Sir Rowland's, will I estate upon you, and here live
   and die a shepherd.

Enter ROSALIND.

ORLANDO   You have my consent. Let your wedding be
   to-morrow: thither will I invite the Duke and all his
   contented followers. Go you and prepare Aliena; for look
   you, here comes my Rosalind.
ROSALIND   God save you, brother.
OLIVER   And you, fair sister.   *[Exit.]*
ROSALIND   O my dear Orlando, how it grieves me to see
   you wear your heart in a scarf!

ORLANDO   It is my arm.

ROSALIND   I thought your heart had been wounded by the claws of a lion.

ORLANDO   Wounded it is, but with the eyes of a lady.

ROSALIND   Did your brother tell you how I counterfeited to swoon when he showed me your handkerchief?

ORLANDO   Ay, and greater wonders than that.

ROSALIND   O, I know where you are! Nay, 'tis true. There was never anything so sudden but the fight of two rams and Caesar's boastful brag of 'I came, saw, and overcame'. For your brother and my sister no sooner met but they looked; no sooner looked but they loved; no sooner loved but they sighed; no sooner sighed but they asked one another the reason; no sooner knew the reason but they sought the remedy. And in these degrees have they made a pair of stairs to marriage, which they will climb incontinent, or else be incontinent before marriage. They are in the very wrath of love, and they will together; clubs cannot part them.

ORLANDO   They shall be married to-morrow, and I will bid the Duke to the nuptials. But, O, how bitter a thing it is to look into happiness through another man's eyes! By so much the more shall I to-morrow be at the height of heart-heaviness, by how much I shall think my brother happy in having what he wishes for.

ROSALIND   Why then, to-morrow I cannot serve your turn for Rosalind?

ORLANDO   I can live no longer by thinking.

ROSALIND   I will weary you then no longer with idle talking. Know of me then, for now I speak to some purpose, that I know you are a gentleman of good intelligence. I speak not this that you should bear a good opinion of my knowledge, insomuch I say I know you are. Neither do I labor for a greater esteem than may in some little measure draw a belief from you, to do yourself good, and not to grace me. Believe then, if you please, that I can do strange things. I have, since I was three years old, conversed with a magician, most

profound in his art and yet not damnable. If you do love
Rosalind so near the heart as your gesture cries it out,
when your brother marries Aliena, shall you marry her.
I know into what straits of fortune she is driven; and it is
not impossible to me, if it appears not inconvenient to
you, to set her before your eyes to-morrow, human as she
is, and without any danger.

ORLANDO   Speak you in sober meanings?

ROSALIND   By my life, I do, which I tender dearly, though
I say I am a magician. Therefore put you in your best
array, bid your friends; for if you will be married to-
morrow, you shall; and to Rosalind, if you will.

Enter SILVIUS *and* PHEBE.

Look, here come a lover of mine and a lover of hers.

PHEBE
Youth, you have done me much ungentleness
To show the letter that I wrote to you.

ROSALIND
I care not if I have. It is my study
To seem despiteful and ungentle to you.
You are there followed by a faithful shepherd:
Look upon him, love him, he worships you.

PHEBE
Good shepherd, tell this youth what it is to love.

SILVIUS
It is to be all made of sighs and tears;
And so am I for Phebe.

PHEBE   And I for Ganymede.

ORLANDO   And I for Rosalind.

ROSALIND   And I for no woman.

SILVIUS
It is to be all made of faith and service;
And so am I for Phebe.

PHEBE   And I for Ganymede.

ORLANDO   And I for Rosalind.

ROSALIND   And I for no woman.

SILVIUS

　It is to be all made of fantasy,
　All made of passion, and all made of wishes,
　All adoration, duty, and observance,
　All humbleness, all patience, and impatience,
　All purity, all trial, all observance;
　And so am I for Phebe.

PHEBE   And so am I for Ganymede.

ORLANDO   And so am I for Rosalind.

ROSALIND   And so am I for no woman.

PHEBE   *[to Rosalind]*

　If this is so, why blame you me to love you?

SILVIUS   *[to Phebe]*

　If this is so, why blame you me to love you?

ORLANDO

　If this is so, why blame you me to love you?

ROSALIND   Why do you speak too, 'Why blame you me
　to love you?'

ORLANDO

　To her that is not here, or does not hear.

ROSALIND   Pray you, no more of this; 'tis like the howling
　of Irish wolves against the moon. *[to Silvius]* I will help
　you if I can. *[to Phebe]* I would love you if I could. To-
　morrow meet me all together. *[to Phebe]* I will marry you
　if ever I marry woman, and I'll be married to-morrow. *[to
　Orlando]* I will satisfy you if ever I satisfied man, and you
　shall be married to-morrow. *[to Silvius]* I will content
　you if what pleases you contents you, and you shall be
　married to-morrow. *[to Orlando]* As you love Rosalind,
　meet. *[to Silvius]* As you love Phebe, meet. And as I love
　no woman, I'll meet. So fare you well, I have left you
　commands.

SILVIUS   I'll not fail if I live.

PHEBE   Nor I.

ORLANDO   Nor I.   *Exeunt.*

SCENE III
Another part of the Forest.

Enter TOUCHSTONE *and* AUDREY.

TOUCHSTONE   To-morrow is the joyful day, Audrey; to-
morrow will we be married.

AUDREY   I do desire it with all my heart; and I hope it is
no dishonest desire to desire to be a woman of the world.
Here come two of the banished Duke's pages.

Enter two PAGES.

FIRST PAGE   Well met, honest gentleman.

TOUCHSTONE   By my word, well met. Come, sit, sit, and
a song!

SECOND PAGE   We are for you. Sit in the middle.

FIRST PAGE   Shall we clap into it roundly, without hawk-
ing or spitting or saying we are hoarse, which are the only
prologues to a bad voice?

SECOND PAGE   In faith, in faith! and both in a tune, like
two gipsies on a horse.

Pages sing.

It was a lover and his lass,
   With a hey, and a ho, and a hey nonino,
That o'er the green cornfield did pass
   In springtime, the only pretty ringtime,
When birds do sing, hey ding a ding, ding.
Sweet lovers love the spring.

Between the acres of the rye,
   With a hey, and a ho, and a hey nonino,
These pretty country folks would lie
   In springtime, &c.

This carol they began that hour,
   With a hey, and a ho, and a hey nonino,

How that a life was but a flower
   In springtime, &c.

And therefore take the present time,
   With a hey, and a ho, and a hey nonino,
For love is crownèd with the prime
   In springtime, &c.

TOUCHSTONE Truly, young gentlemen, though there
was no great matter in the ditty, yet the note was very
untuneable.

FIRST PAGE You are deceived, sir. We kept time, we lost
not our time.

TOUCHSTONE By my word, yes; I count it but time lost
to hear such a foolish song. God be with you, and God
mend your voices. Come, Audrey.   *Exeunt.*

SCENE IV
Another part of the Forest.

Enter DUKE SENIOR, AMIENS, JAQUES, ORLANDO,
OLIVER, CELIA.

DUKE SENIOR
   Do you believe, Orlando, that the boy
   Can do all this that he has promised?

ORLANDO
   I sometimes do believe, and sometimes do not,
   As those that fear they hope, and know they fear.

Enter ROSALIND, SILVIUS, *and* PHEBE.

ROSALIND
   Patience once more, while our compact is urged.
   You say, if I bring in your Rosalind,
   You will bestow her on Orlando here?

DUKE SENIOR
  That would I, had I kingdoms to give with her.
ROSALIND
  And you say you will have her when I bring her?
ORLANDO
  That would I, were I of all kingdoms king.
ROSALIND
  You say you'll marry me, if I am willing?
PHEBE
  That will I, should die the hour after.
ROSALIND
  But if you do refuse to marry me,
  You'll give yourself to this most faithful shepherd?
PHEBE
  So is the bargain.
ROSALIND
  You say that you'll have Phebe, if she will?
SILVIUS
  Though to have her and death were both one thing.
ROSALIND
  I have promised to make all this matter even.
  Keep you your word, O Duke, to give your daughter;
  You yours, Orlando, to receive his daughter.
  Keep you your word, Phebe, that you'll marry me,
  Or else, refusing me, to wed this shepherd.
  Keep your word, Silvius, that you'll marry her
  If she refuses me. From hence I go,
  To make these doubts all even.
                                    Exeunt Rosalind and Celia.
DUKE SENIOR
  I do remember in this shepherd boy
  Some lively touches of my daughter's looks.
ORLANDO
  My lord, the first time that I ever saw him
  I thought he was a brother to your daughter.
  But, my good lord, this boy is forest-born,
  And has been tutored in the rudiments
  Of many dangerous studies by his uncle,

Whom he reports to be a great magician,
Obscurèd in the circle of this forest.

Enter TOUCHSTONE *and* AUDREY.

JAQUES   There is, sure, another flood toward, and these
    couples are coming to the ark. Here comes a pair of very
    strange beasts, which in all tongues are called fools.
TOUCHSTONE   Salutation and greeting to you all!
JAQUES   Good my lord, bid him welcome. This is the
    motley-minded gentleman that I have so often met in the
    forest. He has been a courtier, he swears.
TOUCHSTONE   If any man doubts that, let him put me to
    my purgation. I have trodden a measure; I have flattered
    a lady; I have been politic with my friend, smooth with
    my enemy; I have undone three tailors; I have had four
    quarrels, and like to have fought one.
JAQUES   And how was that taken up?
TOUCHSTONE   Faith, we met, and found the quarrel was
    upon the seventh cause.
JAQUES   How seventh cause? Good my lord, like this
    fellow.
DUKE SENIOR   I like him very well.
TOUCHSTONE   God yield you, sir; I desire you of the like. I
    press in here, sir, among the rest of the country cop-
    ulatives, to swear and to forswear, according as marriage
    binds and blood breaks. A poor virgin, sir, an ill-favored
    thing, sir, but my own; a poor humor of mine, sir, to
    take that that no man else will. Rich honesty dwells
    like a miser, sir, in a poor house, as your pearl in your foul
    oyster.
DUKE SENIOR   By my faith, he is very swift and senten-
    tious.
TOUCHSTONE   According to the fool's bolt, sir, and such
    sweet diseases.
JAQUES   But, for the seventh cause. How did you find the
    quarrel on the seventh cause?
TOUCHSTONE   Upon a lie seven times removed—bear

your body more seeming, Audrey—as thus, sir. I did
dislike the cut of a certain courtier's beard. He sent me
word, if I said his beard was not cut well, he was in the
mind it was. This is called the Retort Courteous. If I sent
him word again it was not well cut, he would send me
word he cut it to please himself. This is called the Quip
Modest. If again, it was not well cut, he disabled my
judgment. This is called the Reply Churlish. If again, it
was not well cut, he would answer I spoke not true. This
is called the Reproof Valiant. If again, it was not well cut,
he would say I lie. This is called the Countercheck
Quarrelsome. And so to the Lie Circumstantial and the
Lie Direct.

JAQUES   And how oft did you say his beard was not well
cut?

TOUCHSTONE   I durst go no further than the Lie Circumstantial, and he durst not give me the Lie Direct; and so
we measured swords and parted.

JAQUES   Can you nominate in order now the degrees of
the lie?

TOUCHSTONE   O sir, we quarrel in print, by the book, as
you have books for good manners. I will name you the
degrees. The first, the Retort Courteous; the second, the
Quip Modest; the third, the Reply Churlish; the fourth,
the Reproof Valiant; the fifth, the Countercheck
Quarrelsome; the sixth, the Lie with Circumstance; the
seventh, the Lie Direct. All these you may avoid but the
Lie Direct, and you may avoid that too, with an If. I knew
when seven justices could not take up a quarrel, but
when the parties were met themselves, one of them
thought but of an If: as, 'If you said so, then I said so'; and
they shook hands and swore brothers. Your If is the only
peacemaker. Much virtue in If.

JAQUES   Is not this a rare fellow, my lord? He's as good at
anything, and yet a fool.

DUKE SENIOR   He uses his folly like a stalking-horse, and
under the presentation of that he shoots his wit.

Enter HYMEN, ROSALIND, *and* CELIA *in their
proper garments. Still music.*

HYMEN   Then is there mirth in heaven
         When earthly things made even
            Atone together.
         Good Duke, receive your daughter;
         Hymen from heaven brought her,
            Yea, brought her hither,
         That you might join her hand with his
         Whose heart within her bosom is.
ROSALIND   *[to Duke]*
   To you I give myself, for I am yours.
      [To Orlando]
   To you I give myself, for I am yours.
DUKE SENIOR
   If there is truth in sight, you are my daughter.
ORLANDO
   If there is truth in sight, you are my Rosalind.
PHEBE
   If sight and shape are true,
   Why then, my love adieu!
ROSALIND   *[to Duke]*
   I'll have no father, if you are not he.
      [To Orlando]
   I'll have no husband, if you are not he.
      [To Phebe]
   Nor ever wed woman, if you are not she.
HYMEN   Peace ho! I bar confusiòn:
            'Tis I must make conclusiòn
               Of these most strange events.
            Here's eight that must take hands
            To join in Hymen's bands,
               If truth holds true contènts.
      [To Orlando and Rosalind]
            You and you no cross shall part.

[To Oliver and Celia]
    You and you are heart in heart.
[To Phebe]
    You to his love must accord,
    Or have a woman to your lord.
[To Touchstone and Audrey]
    You and you are sure together
    As the winter to foul weather.
[To all]
    While a wedlock hymn we sing,
    Feed yourselves with questioning,
    That reason wonder may diminish
    How thus we met, and these things finish.

HYMEN *and attendants sing.*

Wedding is great Juno's crown,
    O blessed bond of board and bed!
'Tis Hymen peoples every town;
    High wedlock then be honorèd.
Honor, high honor, and renown
To Hymen, god of every town!

DUKE SENIOR
    O my dear niece, welcome you are to me,
    Even daughter, welcome, in no less degree!
PHEBE   *[to Silvius]*
    I will not eat my word, now you are mine;
    Your faith my fancy to you does combine.

Enter JAQUES DE BOYS.

DE BOYS
    Let me have audience for a word or two.
    I am the second son of old Sir Rowland
    That bring these tidings to this fair assembly.
    Duke Frederick, hearing now that every day
    Men of great worth resorted to this forest,

Addressed a mighty force, which was on foot
In his own conduct, purposely to take
His brother here and put him to the sword.
And to the skirts of this wild wood he came,
Where, meeting with an old religious man,
After some question with him, was converted
Both from his enterprise and from the world,
His crown bequeathing to his banished brother,
And all their lands restored to them again
That were with him exiled. This to be true
I do engage my life.

DUKE SENIOR   Welcome, young man.
You offer fairly to your brothers' wedding:
To one, his lands withheld; and to the other,
A land itself at large, a potent dukedom.
First, in this forest let us do those ends
That here were well begun and well begot,
And after, every of this happy number
That have endured sharp days and nights with us
Shall share the good of our returnèd fortune,
According to the measure of their states.
Meantime forget this new-fallen dignity
And fall into our rustic revelry.
Play, music, and you brides and bridegrooms all,
With measure heaped in joy, to the measures fall.

JAQUES
Sir, by your patience. If I heard you rightly,
The Duke has put on a religious life
And thrown into neglect the pompous court.

DE BOYS   He has.

JAQUES
To him will I. Out of these convertites
There is much matter to be heard and learned.
   [To Duke]
You to your former honor I bequeath;
Your patience and your virtue well deserve it.
   [To Orlando]
You to a love that your true faith does merit;

    [To Oliver]
You to your land and love and great allies;
    [To Silvius]
You to a long and well-deservèd bed;
    [To Touchstone]
And you to wrangling, for your loving voyage
Is but for two months victualled. So, to your pleasures:
I am for other than for dancing measures.

DUKE SENIOR   Stay, Jaques, stay.

JAQUES
    To see no pastime I. What you would have
    I'll stay to know at your abandoned cave.   *Exit.*

DUKE SENIOR
    Proceed, proceed. We'll begin these rites,
    As we do trust they'll end, in true delights.
                        Exit Music and Dance.

EPILOGUE

ROSALIND It is not the fashion to see the lady the epilogue, but it is no more unhandsome than to see the lord the prologue. If it is true that good wine needs no bush, it is true that a good play needs no epilogue. Yet to good wine they do use good bushes, and good plays prove the better by the help of good epilogues. What a case am I in then, that am neither a good epilogue, and cannot ingratiate on behalf of a good play! I am not furnished like a beggar; therefore to beg will not become me. My way is to conjure you, and I'll begin with the women. I charge you, O women, for the love you bear to men, to like as much of this play as pleases you; and I charge you, O men, for the love you bear to women—as I perceive by your simpering none of you hates them—that between you and the women the play may please. If I were a woman, I would kiss as many of you as had beards that pleased me, complexions that liked me, and breaths that I defied not; and I am sure, as many as have good beards, or good faces, or sweet breaths, will for my kind offer, when I make curtsy, bid me farewell.   *Exit*.